TROY BAYLISS: A FASTER WAY

Troy Bayliss:
A Faster Way

MOTORCYCLE RIDING TECHNIQUES BY THE THREE-TIME WORLD SUPERBIKE CHAMPION

BY TROY BAYLISS WITH ANDREW TREVITT

DESIGN BY TOM MORGAN

DAVID BULL PUBLISHING

Library of Congress Control Number: 2014931707

ISBN: 978 1 935007 22 7

David Bull Publishing, logo, and colophon are trademarks of David Bull Publishing, Inc.

Book and cover design:
Tom Morgan, Blue Design,
Portland, Maine (www.bluedes.com)

Printed in China

10 9 8 7 6 5 4 3 2 1

David Bull Publishing
4250 East Camelback Road
Suite K150
Phoenix, AZ 85018

602-852-9500
602-852-9503 (fax)

www.bullpublishing.com

Photo captions and credits
Pages 2-5 (Courtesy of Ducati)
Page 6: Preparing for practice in the rain at Jerez on the Desmosedici in 2004. (Courtesy of Ducati)
Pages 8-9: Trying to stay warm waiting on the grid at Donington 2007. (Courtesy of Ducati)
Pages 23-25: 1997 - Gold & Goose; 1998 - Double Red; 2000 - Brian J. Nelson (top) / Gold & Goose (bottom); 2003, 2006, 2012 - Courtesy of Ducati

CONTENTS

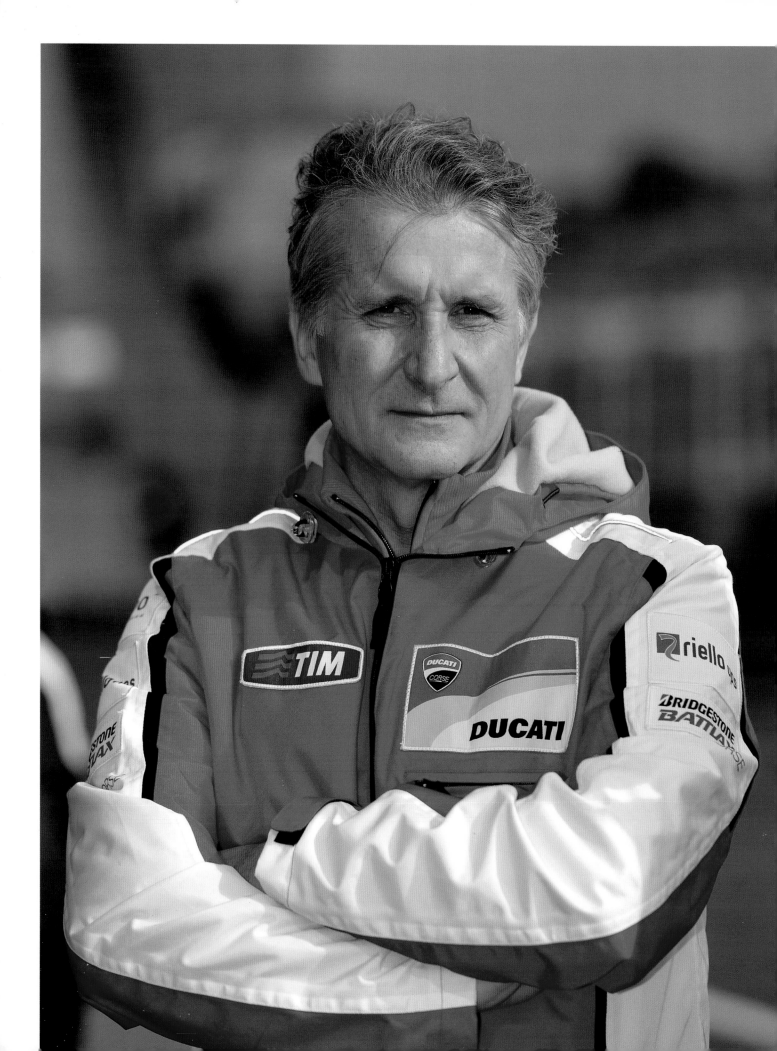

Foreword

BY PAOLO CIABATTI

It gives me great pleasure to have been asked to write the foreword for the book *A Faster Way* because it puts me, so to speak, back on the same page as a rider with whom I have had a very close relationship for well over a decade now, both on and off the track.

I first got to know Troy Bayliss at Daytona in 2000. Before then, despite being Head of Superbike for Ducati Corse, I hadn't really had the chance to meet him or speak to him very much except on the rare occasions he took part in races as a wild-card entrant for the GSE team. At Daytona Troy put in an incredible performance after qualifying in pole position for the first time on an American circuit with banking, racing for the Ducati Vance & Hines team.

Things didn't go as well as we hoped because after leading most of the race, Troy had a mechanical

OPPOSITE: Paolo Ciabatti has had a great influence on my career. When Carl Fogarty crashed in 2000, Paolo, along with Davide Tardozzi and a helmet sponsor of mine, put my name forward to Ducati. He didn't know me very well but I think I was his choice and he pushed for me to ride the bike. Paolo, Davide and Ernesto Marinelli all together were a good crew. There was a lot of passion between those three and they would always come up with a good decision. (COURTESY OF DUCATI) ABOVE RIGHT: Paolo and me on the podium at Monza, Italy, in 2006.

problem and then had to retire due to a crash, but it was afterwards when we, together with his manager Darrell Healey, were analyzing how everything had gone over a glass of beer, that I was able to get a good idea of what truly made this rider tick. Despite having run an extraordinary race at a totally unfamiliar track, he said that he hoped that I wasn't too disappointed by the fact that he hadn't managed to win it....

History then combined to bring us together again for many years following that episode. Troy replaced the injured Carl Fogarty after his crash in Australia and then became the idol of all the *Ducatisti*, winning three World Superbike titles, including two with me, and also winning in an incredible fashion the final MotoGP at Valencia in 2006, when he stood in for the injured Sete Gibernau, and led the race from the start to the chequered flag.

Troy is not just a fantastic rider, he's also a great guy who has a special feeling with everyone he works with and with the Ducati fans. In addition to this, he's also a real pro, a characteristic that is always very useful in this sport. He realized that keeping in perfect shape by following a correct training routine, especially for someone like him who started racing quite late on in life compared to the new generation of riders, was absolutely essential for winning.

I believe that Troy is the rider and person who is most qualified to give advice and suggestions to all those motorcyclists who want to improve their style, and for sure to ride better or quicker; but always in conditions of utmost safety, because his experience in Superbike and in MotoGP, together with his talent, have helped to make him become a true ambassador for bikes in general.

Troy is an unusual, naturally-gifted rider and has a style that seems aggressive but is actually very efficient. He has always used a set-up that is different from that of other riders, but with this set-up he managed to have total control over the bike in every condition, and for this reason his riding sensitivity is exactly what he can transmit through the pages of this book with his advice.

Troy Bayliss is a typical, no-nonsense Australian with a down-to-earth approach about riding, racing and life in general so I hope you get as much pleasure out of reading this book as I did working with him over the years.

Paolo Ciabatti
Ducati Corse Sporting Director

Introduction

When I rode on a race track for the very first time with my Kawasaki KR1 250, I knew I had a natural talent for it. Within a couple of corners I had my knee on the deck, and right away I felt quite fast. I was lucky to turn that natural talent into three World Superbike Championships, but it wasn't easy; I was working on improving my riding from that very first day on the track, right up until my last race at Portimão in 2008.

With this book, I'm hoping to pass on to you what I learned along the way, so that you can ride faster on the track, and safer on the street, without having to go through the mistakes people make and the crashes they have while trying to learn on their own. This book will guide you through the techniques required to ride smoother, faster, and safer, from basic skills such as countersteering and line selection right through to more-advanced skills, like some of the race craft that I used when racing against riders like Noriyuki Haga and Colin Edwards.

Whether you are a street rider looking to be smoother and safer on your weekend rides, a track-day rider hoping to lap quicker than your mates at the next event, or a club-racing MotoGP hopeful, you can benefit from actively improving your riding. And whether the end result is a smooth run down your favorite canyon road or standing on top of the podium, it's a satisfying experience when you make those improvements. Best of all, the riding skills you learn will stay with you. While expensive, sticky race tires and high-horsepower engines have a definite shelf life and need to be constantly replaced, once you learn something such as trail braking (gradually releasing the brakes as the bike is turned in), you will always be able to do it, and you will only get better at it with time and practice.

Many riders think that they are as quick as they'll ever be, and because of that don't even bother working on their riding. Others think that they are "fast" and beyond learning anything from another rider, let alone from reading a book. But the most important thing to realize about motorcycle riding is that it's a

OPPOSITE: Some riders work to improve their riding in order to win races and championships. Other riders want to be faster than their friends at a track day, or simply ride down their favorite road without putting a wheel wrong. Whatever your reason is for wanting to ride better, when everything comes together and you make an improvement, it is a very satisfying experience. **(COURTESY OF DUCATI)**

dynamic skill—you will always be able to improve or change something to be faster, smoother, and safer. This is why I say *fast;* it's a relative term. The hotshot at your local track day may be fast, but how fast is he compared to Max Biaggi or Jorge Lorenzo? How often does he crash? How smooth is he?

There is always room for improvement, and even riders such as Biaggi and Lorenzo are constantly working to go faster on the track. If you've picked up this book, you already know that, so congratulations—you've taken the first step toward improving your riding.

One of the great things about motorcycle riding is that it's an all-encompassing activity with many different facets. People who want to learn more will never lack for something to focus on. In addition, all of these aspects are interconnected and complementary: The physical and mental work together, your natural talent combines with what you learn over time, and what you practice on the track carries over to riding on the street.

This, however, makes things a bit difficult as far as learning how to ride better. If everything is interconnected, in what order should you learn things? Obviously, you will need some basic building blocks in place before learning the advanced techniques. For example, before you can work on trail braking, it helps to have braking and steer-

ing—as separate skills—well sorted. As you progress, however, you'll find that something you learn later as part of an advanced technique may change how you do something basic. While the book is laid out in a general order of basic techniques to the more advanced, you may find yourself checking back or even skipping ahead for this reason. The chapters are best read and digested in order, but each stands on its own, so you can refer back to them later when working on something more specific.

While virtually all of my experience comes from riding on the track, most of the skills and techniques presented here transfer directly to the street; riding a motorcycle is riding a motorcycle, after all. That is not to say you should ride as fast on the street as you do on the track. On the track, racers are concerned mostly with putting in the quick lap times and winning the race. An occasional crash is practically a given at the highest levels, as riders tread that fine line, looking for hundredths of a second in lap times. The goal or focus here is heavily biased toward speed; infrequent crashes are an acceptable risk. Taking a step back, there are no trophies at the end of a track day (and you most likely have a job to go to the next day), so the focus there should be somewhat less on outright speed. A crash is a less-acceptable risk, but certainly may happen if you are experimenting with

BELOW: This data acquisition chart, provided by Ernesto Marinelli from his computer, shows my data for a lap at Phillip Island on the 999. From top to bottom are throttle position (purple), brake pressure (red), speed (black), and gear position (red). **(COURTESY OF DUCATI)**

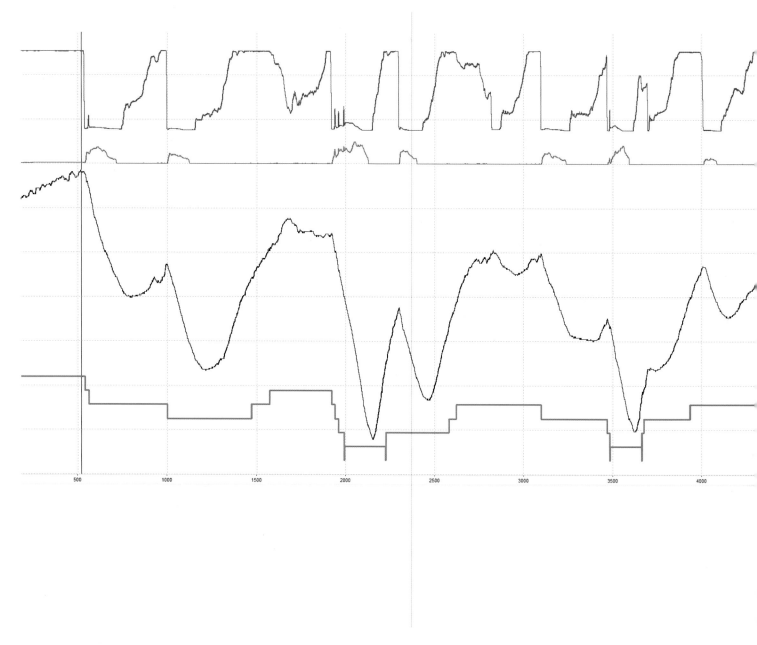

new techniques. At the far end of the spectrum, street riders should be wholly focused on safety, to the point where a crash is unacceptable no matter what the circumstances. Your speed will be determined by things like road conditions and traffic rather than simply how fast you can go.

Improving your riding skills has a double benefit for street riders: Not only will you be a safer rider in terms of reducing the risk of crashing on your own, but you will also be better able to focus on the traffic and conditions around you, in turn further reducing the risk of getting into an accident. Anytime you are trying to learn a new skill or experimenting with a technique you haven't used before, though, there is an increased risk of crashing. If you are making a conscious effort to improve your riding, it's best to go to the race track to practice the techniques in this book. Only there can you devote the concentration necessary to your actual riding rather than worrying about driveways and stray dogs. What you are aiming for as a street rider is to make your skills second nature so you don't have to concentrate on them so much—there are more important things to worry about.

While I was never really a telemetry person, and especially didn't like looking at other people's data, it's useful for learning and can really make some things clear. If you have access to a data acquisition system (such as the Ducati Data Analyzer or a GPS lap timer), it's well worth using. I will refer to this chart several times throughout the book, as there are some definite things to look for in your own data with regard to each skill. It's also a good tool for keeping track of your progress, as you can actually see improvements in the data over time.

Another consequence of motorcycling being so all-encompassing is that, when it comes to many of the skills, there is no right or wrong. If you have your own style or a particular way of doing something, then you shouldn't feel obliged to blindly change what you do to match something explained here. But by the same token, I'd like you to at least try what's shown if you do come across something you don't agree with, as you may find that it's an improvement. Valentino Rossi uses four fingers on the front brake lever, but in Chapter 5, on braking, I will talk about why I think using two fingers is best. Is Valentino wrong? Of course not. But that doesn't mean one

Your riding skill is something that can always be improved. Even at the world championship level, new bikes, tires, and parts meant that I was constantly making adjustments to my riding techniques, right up until I retired in 2008. **(COURTESY OF DUCATI)**

way or the other will work better for you. When it comes down to it, whatever works for you and gets the job done is the correct way. And Valentino certainly gets the job done!

Finally, always remember that riding motorcycles is fun, and that's why we do it. If you have difficulty with a particular chapter or get frustrated trying to change a bad habit, simply set it aside for a while and work on something else. The 12 chapters of

riding techniques in this book will give you plenty of material to work on independently of what's giving you difficulty, and you can easily go back and have a fresh go at it later.

ABOVE: There is no right or wrong way when it comes to many riding techniques, and here is a perfect example: Valentino Rossi has always used four fingers on the front brake, when most other riders use two. What are the benefits of each, and who is right? **(COURTESY OF DUCATI)**

TROY BAYLISS BIOGRAPHY

In an era when the trend is for roadracers to start earlier and earlier in life, Troy didn't start racing on pavement until he was well into his twenties. Even still, in a career spanning 16 years, he won three World Superbike Championships, the British Superbike Championship, and a MotoGP race, setting numerous records along the way.

THE EARLY YEARS

Troy was born on March 30, 1969, in New South Wales, Australia. He started riding motorcycles at the age of six, and racing motocross and dirt track at 10. He raced for four years, but then turned his attention to surfing and competitive cycling. It wasn't until 1992, when Troy was 23 years old, that he purchased his first street bike, a Kawasaki ZXR750 H1. After just two months on the street with the Kawasaki, he realized that he had to get to the track—or risk being put in jail or having a big crash. The ZXR got traded in for a KR1, and then a 600, and Troy was soon winning club and national races in the Sports Production classes. In the next two years, Troy raced the 600 in the Australian National Championship, winning a race and finishing third in the championship in 1995.

AUSTRALIA

In 1996 Troy competed in the Australian Superbike Championship, finishing third in the series with the backing of Kawasaki. The next year he moved to the Suzuki team, finishing second in the series. Entered as a wild card in the Phillip Island round of the World Superbike series, Troy

1998

finished fifth in both legs, his first WSB championship points. This led to another wild-card entry, this time in the Phillip Island Grand Prix World Championship event on the Suzuki RGV250. Troy finished sixth in that race, attracting the attention of the GSE Ducati team in England.

1997

GREAT BRITAIN

Moving to England for two years, Troy competed in the British Superbike Championship for Team GSE Ducati, finishing eighth in 1998. After a year of learning the Ducati and the unique British tracks, Troy won the championship in 1999, with 6 race victories and 14 podium finishes.

THE UNITED STATES

In 2000, Troy moved to America to ride in the AMA Superbike Championship, again for a Ducati team, this time Vance & Hines. Showing immediate speed he qualified on pole in the first two

2000

events; a crash in the first round at Daytona and cancellation of the second round in California prevented Troy from showing his true speed, but then the phone rang . . . .

THE WORLD
Reigning World Superbike Champion Carl Fogarty had seriously injured himself at the Phillip Island round of that series, and Troy was asked to replace the factory Ducati rider. It took just four rounds for Troy to win his first WSB race, at the Hockenheimring in Germany. He followed that up with a pole position at Laguna Seca in the United States, and another win at Brands Hatch in Great Britain, finishing sixth in the championship despite missing three rounds.

2000

2001
Having learned most of the tracks in the series in 2000, Troy put in a dominating performance in 2001 on his way to his first WSB championship, starting the season with five podium performances in a row and his first World Superbike double victory at Monza in Italy. With a total of 6 victories and 15 podium finishes for the year, Troy wrapped up the title one round early with another double victory at Assen in the Netherlands.

2002
Troy continued his dominating performance into the beginning of the next year, winning the first 6 races and an incredible 14 victories in the first 9 rounds. However, a strong performance by his main rival Colin Edwards in the latter part of the season led to their epic battle at the final round in Imola, Italy, where Edwards narrowly beat Troy for the title.

2003

2003
The factory Ducati team, along with Troy, moved to MotoGP for 2003. Despite their newcomer status in the series, it wasn't long before they proved competitive, with Troy on the podium at the third round in Jerez, Spain. He visited the podium twice more in the season, finishing sixth in the championship.

2004

A difficult year on the fast but ill-handling Desmosedici resulted in just one podium finish at Valencia in Spain—the final race of the season—and 14th in the MotoGP standings for the year.

2005

Moving to the Honda MotoGP team for 2005, Troy showed early-season promise but broke his arm badly midway through the year, and missed the final six rounds.

2006

2006

Returning to the factory Ducati World Superbike team, Troy was immediately competitive, opening the season with two podium finishes at the first round in Qatar, and scoring eight victories in a row beginning with the second race of the next round in Phillip Island, Australia. Troy won a total of 12 races and visited the podium 16 times, clinching the title with one round remaining, and ending almost 100 points ahead of James Toseland in the championship. At the end of the year, Troy entered the final MotoGP race at Valencia in Spain as a wild card, and won the race in dramatic, flag-to-flag fashion.

2007

Again on the factory Ducati WSB team, Troy was injured early in the year at Donington Park in England, but still managed to finish fourth in the World Superbike standings, with 7 victories and 13 podium finishes.

2008

In another dominating year on the way to his third WSB championship, Troy led the points table from start to finish, with 11 victories and 19 podium visits. Even though he wrapped up the title with one round remaining, he put a final stamp on the year—and his World Superbike career—by taking a double victory in the final round at the new Portimão circuit in Spain. The final tally for Troy's World Superbike career is 3 championships, 26 pole positions, 52 victories, and 94 podium finishes in 152 races.

PRESENT DAY

After living in Europe for much of his career, Troy has moved back to Australia, where he lives with his wife, Kim, and their three children in Queensland. He still works closely on street bike and race bike development with the Ducati factory, keeps fit with plenty of cycling, and stays active in rider training with the Ducati Riding Experience in Italy, and his own Troy Bayliss Academy in Australia.

2012

CHAPTER 1:
The Rider

Before we work on any actual riding skills, I think it's important to understand the role of the non-riding aspects involved, and how they can directly and indirectly improve your riding. In other words, we want to make sure that you are making full use of the skills you already have, and that, in the future, you can fully utilize each new skill you learn. Not only do you have to walk properly before you try to run, but you also need to wear the right shoes and have a clear path to run on.

The rider equation can be broken down into three components: The *physical aspect*, the *mental aspect*, and the *environment and people* you surround yourself with. For example, if you're going to work on an advanced skill such as trail braking, it's a given that you want to have the basic skill of straight-line braking down solid. On top of that, the brakes on your bike have to be in top condition (part of your environment). You'll need to be fresh, not tired after a long day in the saddle (a physical aspect). And you'll have to be thinking clearly about the braking drill, not about your date the night before (a mental aspect).

Everyone from the novice street rider to the professional racer can benefit from maximizing these three components, and you'll find that they become more and more important as you improve over time. You'll have to be in better and better physical shape as you improve your riding in order to fully use more-advanced skills. The mental side plays an increasingly important role, especially in racing. And the further you work to progress as a rider, the more you will find yourself relying on the expertise of the people and resources around you.

For me, racing in the World Superbike Championship, that meant being in the best physical shape possible; in addition, I was concentrating on each upcoming race long beforehand in order to prepare myself mentally. And on the Ducati team, I had surrounded myself with the best engineers and technicians available. At the highest levels of racing, riding skill and raw talent are important, but just as

OPPOSITE: Here's the goal: Before you even turn a wheel, you must be as mentally and physically prepared as possible, and know that you and your "team" have put the best bike possible underneath you. Whether the ride is a quick trip down to the corner store, a track-day session, or a world championship race, the same thing applies. This will allow you to make full use of the skills you have at any given point in your development as a rider. (COURTESY OF DUCATI)

BELOW: Being comfortable on your bike helps with both the physical and mental aspects of riding; not only does that mean being comfortable from an ergonomic point of view, but you should also be comfortable with the setup you choose, and how it makes your bike handle. When I returned to the Ducati World Superbike team after three years in MotoGP, we actually used some settings from the 998 I rode in 2002 to help with making me comfortable on the 999. (COURTESY OF DUCATI)

OPPOSITE: I first worked with Ernesto Marinelli (here with me at Imola in 2006) in America, in 2000. I wanted to take him with me to the factory team later that year, but it wasn't possible, nor was it possible when I moved to MotoGP. The people I worked with through those years were great, but when I worked with Ernesto again, in 2006 on the 999, straightaway it was the best feeling I'd ever had. We won the championship that year, and that's when we went back on the GP bike and had the win at Valencia. (COURTESY OF DUCATI)

important—maybe even more so—is how well you can manage these aspects off the bike.

That said, all this applies to street riders and track-day riders as well as racers. The more clear your mind is on a Monday-morning commute, the more concentration you can devote to the traffic around you, resulting in a safer ride. If you're in good shape, you can take full advantage of the on-track time at a track day, rather than sitting out the last sessions because you've worn yourself out. Being able to ride to the best of your abilities whenever you throw a leg over your bike will pay off in many ways. Not only will it allow you to ride more safely

on the street or faster on the track at any given time, but you will also find that your riding skill improves much faster when you are not limiting yourself in other ways.

From both a physical and mental point of view, one of the most important things that I've found over the years is that you have to be comfortable on the bike. This means having the controls positioned properly for you, and the setup of the bike to your liking. It's difficult to ride your best on the track if you are constantly distracted by something about the bike setup, and this can affect both the mental and physical sides of your riding. When journalists or other racers rode any of my race bikes, they were always surprised at how comfortable they were. It was never what they expected—a harsh buckboard set on its nose with little feeling—but rather a nice, comfortable easy chair, as I like to call it.

In 2006, I returned to the factory Ducati team after a year on the Honda MotoGP bike. When I rode the 999 for the first time, the bike worked well right away, but didn't feel like "my" bike. We changed the settings and used the head angle and offset from the 998 I rode in 2002, and immediately, I was more comfortable. This was my lounge chair, the bike I was used to, all set and ready to go; it almost felt like I could just put my feet up and enjoy the ride. It may not have been the

Sometimes a race can be mentally as well as physically exhausting. At Misano, for example, when you are
riding so close to one another in the heat, it can be
difficult to breathe because it's so hot, and you're so
close to other riders, with their bikes' exhaust right in
your face. Getting yourself through that can be really
hard, but you just have to tell yourself that you can get
through the race. Here, I'm dicing with Noriyuki Haga,
Troy Corser, and Max Biaggi for the lead in race 1 at
Misano in 2007. The temperature that day, typical for
Misano, was 31 degrees Celsius (88 degrees Fahrenheit), with 38 percent humidity. **(COURTESY OF DUCATI)**

quickest bike around the track for a single lap, but this setup made it less taxing on me physically to ride two long races in a day—more important when it comes to actually *winning* races—and it made it simply more fun to ride as well.

We will delve into the mental and physical aspects individually in Chapter 9. However, as you go through the rest of this book, consider the mental and physical facets of each skill as they are presented. It's also worth considering how the two are intertwined. For example, you could beef up your arm strength to go faster through a particular chicane at your favorite race track—or, you could come up with a different line that doesn't require that the bike be turned as quickly. Or you could do both, of course. Some skills, such as vision and reference points, are completely mental in nature, while others—such as body position—are all physical. The majority, however, have components of each in some combination, so think of the requirements of each skill from both a physical and mental standpoint.

Many riders, by nature or by choice, make the mistake of favoring the physical aspect over mental, or vice versa, and this can lead to wasted effort. If you are naturally big and strong, it's not likely that going to the gym every day will help your riding as much as studying some onboard video or going to a yoga class. On the other hand, it's no use flailing around the track trying to work on something if you are worn out halfway through the session. Your own strengths and weaknesses in each area will determine where much of your effort should be concentrated, and constant reevaluation will help you to determine what aspects of your riding need work. Again, it all boils down to maximizing the skills and attributes you *already have* before attempting to improve any particular skill.

The third part of the rider equation is your environment, which is mostly represented by the team of people you assemble around you. This is another key aspect that applies not just to racers; track-day riders have an increasing amount of support at their disposal, as do street riders. At my level of racing, the team is a crucial part of the result; the importance of having people you trust on your side cannot be underestimated.

For example, at Ducati I always relied on Alessandra Balducci, my electronics engineer. She was incredible when it came to the mapping of the bike, something I was fanatical about. I always wanted it smooth when the bike was really leaned over and I first opened the throttle; that was the main thing we used to work on. She knew what I was looking for the whole time, and knew how important it was to me. Knowing that I had someone like Alessandra putting that much effort into such a minute detail of my program made me put that much more effort in myself. The other aspects of the bike—suspension, chassis, tires, and so on—all play just as important a role, and for each you need someone who understands you, someone you can believe in 100 percent, knowing they are doing everything possible for you.

For these reasons, it's every bit as important for club racers and even track-day riders to put together their own team of trusted people. Certainly it depends on your resources and how elaborate your racing plans are, but even if you are just going to a track day for fun, it's worthwhile having a friend come along to look after your bike for you. At the track you'll find vendors more than happy to help you with tires, suspension setup, or even a complete race-ready bike to ride. Even if all your friend does is keep your bike gassed up and your visor clean, then those are two fewer things you'll have to worry about.

Street riders, of course, won't have a small army of factory engineers looking after their bikes, but there are resources you can access. Your local dealer is a good place to start if you have questions or need help with bike preparation or setup. There are loads of Internet sites with good information. Or help may come in the form of a how-to book. It may be something as simple as being your own "mechanic" the night before a ride, making sure your bike is prepped and ready to go, so that you can switch into "rider" mode the next day and not be distracted by having to work on your bike.

Note that the level of help you get will depend largely on how much effort you put into your own program. Just as Alessandra's hard work spurred

BELOW: Celebrating Ducati's 250th World Superbike win at Brands Hatch in 2006. At the top levels, the race teams are staffed with dozens of people responsible for many different aspects, from managing the spare-parts supply to driving the transporter. Your own "team" may only consist of a couple of friends helping to put gas in the bike and clean your face shield for a weekend club race, but they are every bit as important to your success as a racer, and your ongoing improvement as a rider. **(COURTESY OF DUCATI)**

me on to try even harder, I'm sure that she put a lot of that effort in because she saw how hard I worked at it, and there was a positive snowball effect there. Whether you're on a big team like I was, or on your own with a friend at a track day, the same thing applies. Your friend is likely to go the extra mile if he or she sees you rehydrating and thinking about your riding in between sessions rather than off having a laugh with your mates. A suspension vendor will give you extra attention if you roll up on a clean motorcycle and pay attention to and ask questions about the adjustments made. People will naturally be more inclined to help you when they see you putting in the hours yourself.

These people and your environment all tie into the mental and physical side of the overall picture: The more load you can take off yourself, having someone you trust to look after things, the more it will free you up to concentrate on your riding; in turn, this allows you to relax and conserve your energy. Unfortunately, the harsh reality of motorcycle racing is that it's very difficult to get that help, even for top-level national

racers. Many club racers and track-day riders fall into the trap of working so hard to put their program together—building their own bikes, driving all over the country, and working their fingers to the bone at the track—that attention to the mental and physical aspects of their riding fall by the wayside. Working a 60-hour week to build an ultrafast bike won't help you if you're half asleep on the grid.

It's all a matter of balance—no matter what level you're at—and the amount of time you devote to each aspect will change as your riding develops. With each new skill you learn, evaluate where it fits into your toolbox, and whether you need to make any changes. It may be something physical, like needing more leg strength to properly use body steering; something mental, such as having better reference points for braking; or it may be something in your environment, such as asking someone to help you with your suspension before you tackle corner sequences. Focus on achieving this balance, and you will be better prepared to fully use a given skill, along with learning the next one.

CHAPTER 2:
Visual Skills

O f all the corners on all the tracks I've ridden over the years, I've always thought that Dingle Dell—now called Sheene's Corner—at Brands Hatch in England is one of the most difficult to get right. After going through a huge dip in the track, you have to be turning into the apex while still going uphill, well before you can actually see the corner. And then when you crest the hill—while still in the corner—there is no weight on the bike at all. That whole section of the circuit is difficult. When I went there in BSB (British Superbike) and rode that part for the first time, there were guys passing me and I was thinking, "How are they doing this?" A lot of the English guys at the time were pretty special at it.

Of course, what makes Dingle Dell so troublesome is that it's a blind corner, and you can't see where you are going. Many riders, at all levels, have difficulty with this, and it shows just how important

visual skills are when it comes to riding a motorcycle. There is no way to see around a blind corner or over a hill, but working on visual techniques can help in these and other tricky situations when you're riding.

There are loads of things to see in your field of vision while riding a motorcycle; essentially, you want to train yourself to "look" at one thing while you actually "see" and concentrate (or focus) on another. Football players and other athletes are perfect examples of this: An expert player will be watching the ball but will know exactly where all the other players are at any given time. And jugglers take this to the extreme, looking at a single point in the distance and never directly at what they are juggling.

The most important aspect of your vision is to keep your eyes up and looking far ahead. This has the effect of slowing things down and making it easier for you to process what you see. While you are riding your bike or driving in a car on an empty stretch of straight road, look down at the tarmac right beside you. Note how little you can actually see and how fast it is rushing by; you can hardly pick out any single characteristic or spot on the road, let alone decide what to do about it. Now look up and far away to the side. Note now how much more you can see,

OPPOSITE: Ensure that you can easily see as much as possible by using a clean visor that is in good condition, along with a clear shield at night or on a cloudy day. The windscreen on your bike should also be clear, with no distortion when you look through it. (COURTESY OF DUCATI)

and how much slower it appears to be moving past you. You can easily pick something out and focus on it for an extended length of time. Don't forget to concentrate on your riding or driving while you're doing this, of course!

While it may seem obvious, another benefit of looking up and far ahead is that you can see where you are going. A natural instinct for some riders is to look at the road directly in front of them, as they consider that to be where they are going. But the reality is that if you see something on the road 5 or even 10 feet from your front tire, you will be unable to react in time to do anything about it. Looking far ahead allows you to plan equally far ahead, giving you more time to think about the corner coming up, or what that car in the intersection may do in the next few seconds.

So, with your eyes up and in general looking far ahead to where you are going, what should you actually try to see and concentrate on? At any time on the race track or on the road, you want to have something that helps you know exactly where you are and what you should be doing—be it a stripe in the road, a curb marking an apex, or a tree off in the distance. These are *reference points*, something we'll explore in more detail in Chapter 8; for now, the goal is to learn how to scan the road ahead for these points, as well as any potential danger or changing conditions, and then track those items with your peripheral vision while you continue to scan ahead. Track riders will obviously be more concerned with reference points (as conditions and the track will rarely change), while street riders will focus more on traffic and seeing where the road actually goes.

This is something you can practice and work on at home, or at almost any time and during any activity. Start by sitting in a chair facing a wall that is at least 3 meters (10 feet) away and has some items on it that you can concentrate on, such as pictures or furniture. While keeping your gaze on a point straight ahead of you, shift your focus—but not your eyes—to one of the nearby objects. This is your peripheral vision at work. Try and pick out as much detail as you can without actually looking at it. What is it? What color and shape is it? Move your focus back to where you are actually looking, and then to another object a bit farther away than the first. Keep going, moving your focus back and forth between the spot on the wall and other objects progressively farther away.

You will find that as you work farther and farther away from the spot directly ahead on the wall, it gets more and more difficult to keep your gaze on the spot directly ahead. At the extreme, when you are trying

BELOW: When riding, your gaze should be on a point well down the road or track, continually scanning for reference points or potential danger spots. Use your peripheral vision to track those items as they get closer, without actually looking at them. **(GOLD & GOOSE)**

to focus on something directly to the side, it's very difficult *not* to pull your eyes away from where you are looking. Unfortunately, this is exactly what we must do with many reference points. If you are using something right beside the track, such as a braking marker, you must be able to focus on it from the time you first see it to the moment you are right beside it, all without actually looking directly at it.

At Phillip Island, for example, there are no marker boards for turn 1. They put them up sometimes, but not always. There are, however, two white lines on the track, at about 100 meters and 50 meters. I use these for my braking markers, depending on the engine in my bike, my drive off the last corner, and the wind conditions. The superbikes are easily going more than 300 kph (185 mph) at that point, and at those speeds, you simply cannot look down at the track to see something—the corner is coming up so fast. I watch for the lines as soon as I'm on the straight and know where they are, but I never actually look at them.

You can work on picking out and identifying something at the side of the road while driving or riding on the highway. Again, choose an empty stretch of straight road, with as little traffic as possible. Keep your gaze as far ahead on the road as possible, and focus on a sign or tree right beside the road in the distance. Keep your concentration on that object as you get closer to it and eventually pass, but try not to look directly at it. Peripheral vision is better at detecting motion than a stationary object, and you may find it actually easier to follow the object as it gets closer and moves faster, relative to you.

Just as important as knowing what to look at and focus on is knowing what *not* to look at or focus on. When you are on the track or a winding road with other riders, you cannot let them distract you from what you are doing. You may have to effectively look right through them to keep your gaze on the road ahead, and yet you must also occasionally focus on them to note what they are doing. The first corner on the first lap of a race is always a busy place; riders are all around, and you have to watch what they are doing while still focusing on your own riding. Monza especially was a place with an especially difficult first corner before the layout was changed, as it was quite a tight corner after a long straight. It was a place that always brought on a first-corner accident in a race, and you had to be on your toes. It was always nice to be able to see a tiny bit out of the corner of my eye, just so I knew where everybody was to avoid getting into any trouble.

This is another aspect of your vision that you can work on away from the race track or twisty roads. While riding, keep your gaze up and far ahead on the road and pick out as much information about the cars around you as you can without looking directly at them. Work toward focusing on a car right beside you while still looking ahead. What kind of car is it? What color is it? What is the driver doing? This skill will come in handy dodging traffic in the city as much as it will when it comes to outbraking another rider on the race track.

Having that control of your vision and being able to focus on more than one thing at once goes a long way toward eliminating target fixation, which is something many riders—even experienced riders—often have trouble with. *Target fixation* is a natural reaction in a panic situation; we instinctively stare and focus on the source of danger with tunnel vision, to the exclusion of everything else. In many situations, this results in automobile drivers, motorcyclists, bicyclists, and even pilots running right into the very thing they were trying to avoid.

For street riders this is a common problem, as they have the added difficulty of traffic and obstacles to deal with. By focusing on a car that pulls out in front of you or a patch of gravel that suddenly appears around a corner, you can target-fixate on the car or gravel and run right into it. If you do come across such a situation, the correct reaction is to find a safe escape route and look directly where you want to go; use your peripheral vision to keep track of where the obstacle is, while your main focus and vision is on the path to safety.

I see target fixation quite a lot with the newer guys on the race track, the young chargers coming through. Often they outbrake themselves and run wide into a corner. Instead of keeping their eyes up and looking *through* the corner, they look directly at the edge of the track—the source of danger—and then target-fixate on it and run right off. The same thing can happen in a blind corner, such as Dingle Dell at Brands Hatch. Because the corner is blind and the track goes over a hill, you can't even see a point far ahead to look at. The natural instinct is to look at and concentrate on something you can actually see, leading to target fixation. Even though you may only be able to see a few dozen meters ahead, keep your eyes up and your gaze as far down the track as you can see, or even on an imaginary point in the distance that corresponds to where your next reference point will be when it comes into view.

LEFT AND BELOW: Blind corners, or turns that crest a hill, are difficult because you cannot see where you want to go. The turn at the top of the hill here is Dingle Dell, at Brands Hatch; you can see how steep it is from the view looking down from the top. Riders must turn into the corner without being able to see the apex or the exit. Our natural instinct is to find at least something to look at, and in the absence of anything far away, we focus on what is close by. Keep your gaze as far up the track or road as you can, or on a point that corresponds to your next reference point when it comes into view. **(GOLD & GOOSE)**

Good vision techniques help in two ways when it comes to target fixation: First, by keeping your eyes up and looking far ahead on the street or track, it's less likely that you'll ever get into a panic situation and have to worry about target fixation. And second, if things do get out of hand, looking directly at and focusing on where you want to go will naturally help you move away from the danger.

As you can imagine, there are some environmental factors to consider when it comes to your vision. It's imperative that your helmet shield and the windscreen on your bike are in good condition and clean at all times. The windscreen on your bike should be clear, not tinted or smoked, and have no distortion so that you can see clearly through it when tucked in. Use an appropriate helmet shield for the

conditions—tinted or smoked on sunny days, clear at night or on a cloudy day. When shopping for a helmet, think about your peripheral vision, and check how well you can see out of the sides and top of the helmet's eyeport. Will you be able to see the track ahead if you are in a full tuck? Will the gauges on your bike be visible over the chin bar, without you having to look down?

It's worthwhile to have your vision checked regularly for any changes; normally, Ducati would test its riders every three months, with vision tests included in a really good checkup on our bodies. Eyeglass frames can also interfere with your vision, and you should consider contact lenses if you need corrective eyewear. That said, I knew someone who switched from glasses to contact lenses and had problems with the contacts. It always goes back to whatever's more comfortable for you, which is just as important.

The end goal of managing your vision is to always have your eyes up and your gaze on a point in the distance. While you are "looking" far ahead, you are "seeing" a constant stream of reference points and details in your peripheral vision. This information tells you exactly where you are and what you should be doing, and alerts you to any dangers or changing conditions ahead that may require you to take evasive action.

CHAPTER 3:
Line Selection

Now that you know what you should be looking at, and for, when riding, the next important topic to address is *where* you should be going. To me this is more important than, say, body position or throttle control, because it's a safety issue.

Generally the track is cleaner and has better grip on the proper riding line; if you do make a mistake working on an advanced skill, so long as you are on the correct line, you will at least have the most traction possible to help you recover. That correct line is typically from the outside of the track at the entry and tipping the bike in toward an apex, which is a point at roughly the center of the turn. If something happens in the middle of the corner—and that's usually where it does happen—then you've got a lot of room before you get to the outside. If,

however, you're off-line right at the outside with a lot of lean angle and something goes wrong, you've got no room to spare.

A lot of riders get stuck on taking a picture-perfect, classic, outside-inside-outside line all the time, but really, every corner is different, and there is no perfect line. Different riders have different styles; different bikes and setups can affect your line in a corner; and camber, elevation, and even bumps can change where you go in a particular turn. I've found the best way to learn the quickest lines on the track is to follow other riders and see what works and what doesn't. It's the easiest way to see the general line and the apex for each corner, and from there you can experiment to discover what works best for you and your setup. Of course, putting it all together and getting it all correct is the difficult part!

I was always learning new lines from other riders and trying different things—anything to gain even a little bit of an advantage. At Assen, there is a really fast, right-to-left transition before the last chicane; it's still there on the new layout. In 2001, I was losing a lot of time to Ruben Xaus through there, so much that it was incredible. I was trying to brake and turn the bike, but what you had to do was go in there

OPPOSITE: Camber and elevation changes in a turn will move your apex earlier or later, as well as your turn-in and exit points. In general, you want to adjust your line to make more of your actual turn on the most uphill or the most banked part of the corner; the banking and slope of the track help you the most here. This is the Corkscrew at Laguna Seca, an extreme example of elevation and camber changes. **(GOLD & GOOSE)**

BELOW: Even the simplest-looking corners have aspects that subtly change the racing line. Camber, elevation, radius, and even bumps can change your line, and there can be a number of lines that work in any particular turn. This is partly why many riders can go to the same track all the time and never get sick of it; they are constantly searching for new lines and ways to "beat" the track. **(COURTESY OF DUCATI)**

OPPOSITE: In this right-left section of track in Qatar, there is just enough of a straight between the two turns for riders on maneuverable 125s to separate the section into individual turns and treat them individually. Riders on heavier and faster superbikes, however, cannot make it back across the track, and must sacrifice the exit of the first turn just slightly to optimize the entrance—and exit—of the second turn. It definitely adds distance to each lap to cross the track like this, but this is more than offset by the extra speed you can carry in each turn. **(GOLD & GOOSE)**

absolutely flat out and just roll off a little bit earlier without touching the brakes; that was just upsetting everything. It's one of those corners where if you try to rush it or go in deeper, it just doesn't work. It can save you so much time by not upsetting the bike. It's a classic case of a turn where what looks like the perfect line is not the best way through the turn.

At the Ducati Riding Experience or my own Academy, I spend a lot of time showing people around the track. It gets them comfortable right away, and—as the old story goes—a lot of going fast is about being comfortable. Many newer riders always seem to ride around like they are on a 125, with way too much corner speed. They wash off only a tiny bit of speed heading into the corner, as they've got no idea how hard they can use the brakes. Then they make the corner much longer than it has to be, and stay on the side of the tire for a long time. I'm behind them thinking they are going really fast—I

wouldn't want to go much faster even! Not only is all that lean angle and corner speed really dangerous for them, it's also really difficult for them to go any faster using that type of line and technique. Usually I try to show those people the line around the track, and then take them for a ride on the two-seater. Then they realize how much brake they can use and how deep they can go into the corner.

The classic racing line for a single corner is from the outside of the track to the inside in the middle of the corner, and then back to the outside on the exit. This gives you the best combination of a big radius to carry corner speed and a short distance to save time. Where you begin your arc into the corner from the outside of the track is called the *turn-in point*. The *apex* is defined as the point where you are closest to the inside of the corner (typically the slowest part); where you end the corner at the outside of the track is the *exit point*.

Using the classic line, these points are well defined, with little room for error. Smaller bikes, like 125cc or Moto3 Grand Prix bikes, can best use this classic line; this is because they can carry the corner speed and don't have to worry so much about braking or accelerating at the entry and exit. On bigger, more powerful bikes, you want to be on the very edge of the tire for as little time as possible, and this calls for

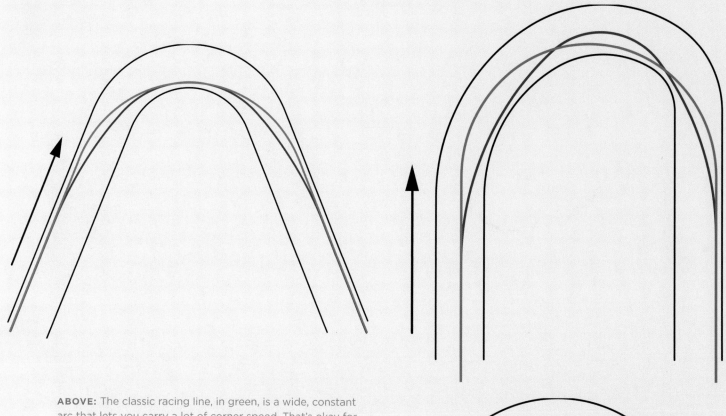

ABOVE: The classic racing line, in green, is a wide, constant arc that lets you carry a lot of corner speed. That's okay for 125s and smaller bikes, as they can make the quick transition necessary from upright to full lean on the entry, and don't have a lot of power to get into trouble on the exit. Larger and more-powerful bikes, however, can make better use of the more-contemporary line, shown in blue, with a tighter arc right at the apex of the corner, trail-braking on the entry with a gradual application of power on the exit.

ABOVE RIGHT: In a corner with a decreasing radius, you will have to use a late apex with the classic line (green) to avoid running out of room at the exit. A more-contemporary line with double apex leaves room on both the entry and exit of the corner. Both lines will require some patience on the entry, as it may seem like you are going too slow in the beginning part of the turn, where the radius is greater. Turns that are downhill or have negative camber require a similar line.

RIGHT: An increasing-radius corner is usually much easier than a decreasing-radius corner, as you can use an early apex, and there is plenty of room on the exit. If you use a classic line (green), you will usually end up accelerating on the edge of the tire for a dangerously long time. Using a contemporary line (blue) moves the apex—where you are going the slowest—to a point later in the turn, and away from the edge of the track. Uphill and banked turns have a similar line to an increasing-radius turn.

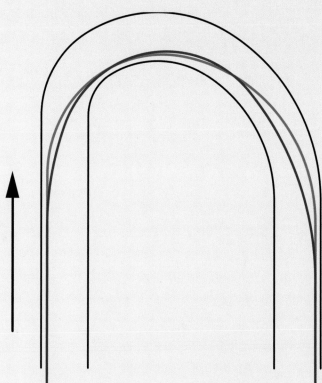

somewhat of a different line. It's a more-gradual entry into the turn, with more trail braking as the bike is leaned over. At the apex, however, the actual radius of the corner is tighter (and the speed a bit slower), but you're leaned right over on the edge for much less time. On the exit, the bike is lifted onto the middle part of the tire earlier, so that you can apply the power and get a good drive down the straight. The turn-in point is earlier than with the classic line, the exit point is later, and the apex can be either earlier or later (this is where a lot of the experimentation comes in).

There are an almost infinite number of variations here. You can go a bit slower in the actual corner and use a later apex so that you can get the bike more upright and accelerating sooner onto a long straight. This would apply if, for example, you were riding a big, heavy bike that didn't handle all that well. The turn may tighten up as you go, with a decreasing radius. There may be elevation changes, where the track goes uphill or downhill, or there may be some camber involved. A corner has *positive camber* if it is banked, with the outside of the turn higher than the inside. The opposite, with the track falling away from you toward the outside, is *negative camber*. Any of these characteristics will cause your entry, exit, and apex points to change, and you may not even use the whole track.

And finally, some bikes work differently than others. You may find you can tip into a corner later than somebody else on a different bike, or the other person's bike may be working better than yours, and it may feel like you have to tip it in earlier. But even then you may find something that helps you on the exit of the corner. There are many different ways around any corner; you don't actually know which is best for you and your bike until you're out on the track with someone else and you can see if a particular line is helping or hindering you.

In car racing, the best line is usually quite clear, and you have to be very precise to be quick, partly because a car is so much wider than a bike. But on a bike it's easier, and you don't have to worry so much about being absolutely perfect and on-line in every corner.

When I first raced in the UK and was in a hurry to learn the tracks, a lot of guys would point out that I was a half-foot or a quarter-foot off-line. I learned that this wasn't really that critical. You don't have to be millimeter-on unless you're trying to beat Valentino or Casey Stoner. It's more important to be

The first few corners of Donington Park in England, including Redgate and Craner Curves, is a perfect example of how several corners can be linked together, as well as the importance of line choice. Exiting Redgate, it seems that you can go faster, but in reality you have to roll off the throttle to help get the bike turned into the first part of Craner Curves, the right-hander at the top of the picture. Overshoot that right, or make one tiny little mistake, and there's a good chance you've messed up the whole section, right through to the Old Hairpin, the corner at the bottom of the picture. **(GOLD & GOOSE)**

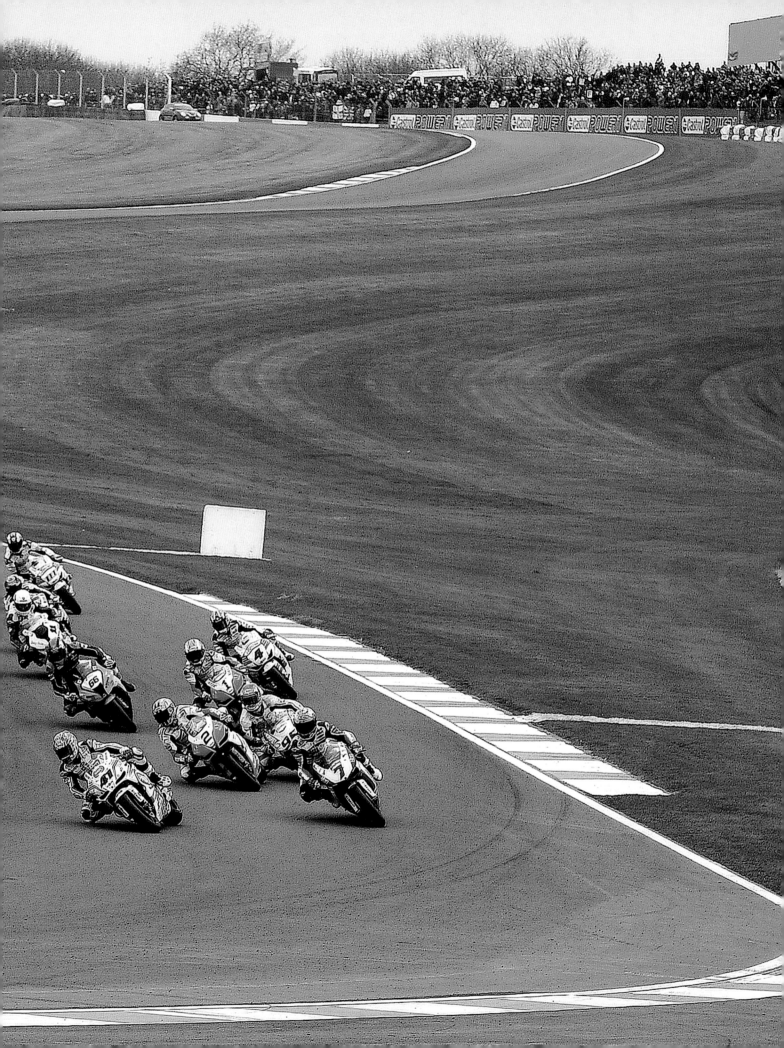

consistent lap to lap so that you can experiment. If you take one corner particularly well on a certain lap, and gain a lot of speed onto the following straight, you want to be able to know exactly what you did differently so that you can repeat it. If you're not consistent in your line, you'll have trouble finding out what works, and why.

The diagrams in this chapter illustrate some of the more-common types of corners and combinations of corners you'll find. Race-track designers can be quite devious, and it's rare that you'll find a simple corner with a constant radius. When two corners are close together, it can get tricky, as there are a lot of elements to consider. Usually, the final corner in a series is the most important, as you want the best drive onto the following straight as you can get. You want to make the most of the exit, so an optimum line through the second turn is crucial.

Working backwards, what do you need to do in the first corner to put yourself at the correct entry point into the second corner? If one of the earlier corners is much faster, you may save more time by using a more-efficient line in that particular corner. You will have to decide where you want to prioritize, and select your entry, apex, and exit points accordingly. One thing to keep in mind: Just because everyone else on the track uses a certain line in a section doesn't mean it's the right line for you. Don't be afraid to experiment and try something different.

Donington Park is a great example of how several corners can be connected into a series. The first corner is Redgate, a right-hand corner, and following that are a downhill right and left: Craner Curves. When you exit Redgate and arc into the right-hand corner of Craner Curves, if you are too aggressive and don't close the throttle enough to help you turn the bike, it just wrecks everything, causing a lot of crashes there.

This has happened to me and many other people over the years; you get in there and you're rushing so hard to turn the bike. What you have to remember is to have some patience and actually slow yourself down by rolling off the gas. Usually, when you want to go faster, you try and do it with the throttle on, but changing direction with a lot of throttle makes it much harder. Here, even though the temptation is to keep accelerating, you've got to roll off the gas to get the bike set up correctly for the corner. And then, if you overshoot that first part by even six inches or a foot, there's no way you can get far enough over to the right side of the track for the left-hand corner. You're trying so hard to get over that you could easily lose the back or the front. Overdoing that first part and rushing into the next part has caused many crashes.

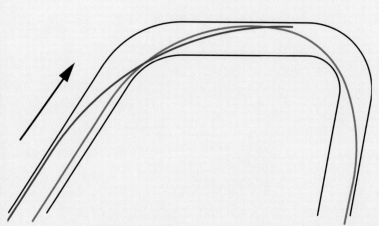

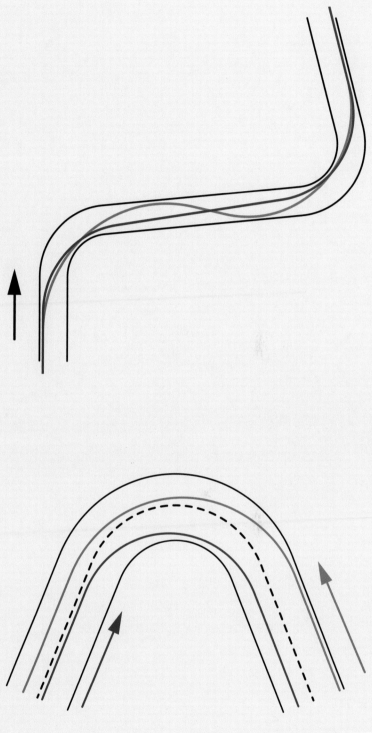

ABOVE: In the combination shown here, you will have to sacrifice something in the first turn in order to be positioned properly at the entry of the second turn. A line taking into account only the first part of the turn, shown here in red, puts you in the wrong place and direction to maximize your speed in the second part. It may be a matter of an earlier apex in the first corner to push you wide to the second corner's entry point, shown here in green. If the corners are very close together, treat the combination as a single, decreasing-radius turn.

ABOVE RIGHT: When the turns in a combination are opposite, as in the chicane shown here, the optimum lines for the individual turns means going from one side of the track to the other in between, shown here in green. That can add a significant distance and time to the section, and it may be quicker overall to take a straighter line between the two turns, shown here in blue. The correct line will be something in between these two extremes; it depends on how close the corners are together, along with many other factors. The best way to find the quickest line is to experiment and compare the results with that of other riders.

RIGHT: Street riders should use lines generally similar to those shown for the race track, with changes to account for traffic and other details. Here it's not a matter of speed, but of safety. Most importantly, you've only got half the road to deal with—even less, since you don't want to lean over the center line and into the other lane at all, and you don't want to use all the road on the exit. Using a later entry and staying to the outside of the lane longer before tipping the bike in serves a double purpose: First, that late entry lets you see farther around the corner, and gives you more warning if there is oncoming traffic or something on the road. And second, that will naturally tighten up your exit line, giving you more room to the edge of the lane should something happen. Properly stitching together a series of turns on the street can be even more difficult than on the track, as there are more elements to consider.

If you do manage to stay on, you've wrecked the left, and then you're too far over to the right of the track to get into the Old Hairpin, the right-hand turn at the bottom. Then you end up wrecking *that*, running out way too wide there, and then you've wrecked the next section to get up through the left under the Starkey's Bridge. That entire section, from when you cross the start/finish straight to the Old Hairpin, is absolutely linked together more than any other track that I know. Trying to learn that place in a hurry when you're trying to go fast is a very difficult thing to do.

In chicanes and combinations of left and right corners, distance is just as important as speed. If you go all the way across the track from one side to the other between two turns to get more corner speed, you are adding a lot of distance. It may be better to straighten out the transition in between the two corners, saving distance, and sacrifice a bit of corner speed.

A perfect example of this is at Imola, in the Variante Alta chicane. I used to actually run over the curb on the right in the first part, just to straight-line it a bit more. Then I wouldn't have to tip it over as much into the right before putting it into the left. Going over the curb definitely slowed me down, but it saved a lot of distance and set me up much better for the second part. They eventually put up cones and told us not to go there, but people would knock them over and go there anyway. If you can get away with it, places like this afford the shortest, and the quickest, way around.

As I say, however, every corner or combination of corners is unique, and ultimately you will have to experiment and compare your lines to other riders, along with all of the inherent advantages and disadvantages. Years after I learned that line at Assen from Ruben Xaus, I had a really big battle there with James Toseland. In 2007 I think I passed him four times in that corner on the inside, in the last four laps of the second race, using the line I'd learned many years before. I was just so much faster through there. Of course, James covered the line on the last lap, but I got him in the chicane to win the race.

There are so many subtle aspects to corners that can change the quickest line, and those aspects can even change over time; there is almost no such thing as a "perfect" line. I am always looking for a faster way around the track, and that means watching the riders around me to see what they are doing, as well as constantly trying different lines on my own.

CHAPTER 4:
Steering

Turning your motorcycle into a corner is one of the simplest and easiest aspects of riding, yet at the same time, it's also one of the most complex and difficult. Most of us have ridden bicycles since we were children, and steering a bicycle or motorcycle is second nature—you just think about what direction you want to go and . . . turn. But if you want to ride your bike quickly around the race track, or more safely on a twisting road, there is much more to it than that. Getting through a fast chicane properly requires all your strength and concentration, as well as a good deal of finesse.

As an example, let's look at the Geert Timmer chicane at Assen, just before the start/finish line. In the transition of the chicane, you want to go from right to left. That means pulling on the right handlebar and pushing on the left. It's a fast chicane, so this takes a lot of effort. At the same time, you're pulling on the throttle a little bit, but as you're doing that, you're also pushing your body over to the

OPPOSITE: On the exit of a turn, you may have to lift the bike up from full lean quickly to get set for the next turn. If you have enough power applied, the front wheel may tuck under. (COURTESY OF DUCATI)

left, really hard off your right foot, to help bring everything over. And you're even pushing forward on the other footpeg, just to make everything happen really fast. It's where you use every part of your body; you're using your arms hard, you're pushing your body over to the left, and you're pushing down on your right footpeg. And when you're coming out of the chicane at Assen, you're already hanging off the bike in another way, trying to help everything. It just takes so much more effort to make everything happen quickly in a fast chicane, and you can see that effort in how top-level racers are completely worn out at the end of a race.

Although this certainly sounds intimidating, you may be surprised at how quickly you can actually steer your bike without all that physical effort. Countersteering is the most effective tool for steering, and it can provide a large portion of the result—turning your bike quickly—with only a moderate level of effort. You can sit completely still on the seat and use only your arms on the bars to steer, and your bike will happily go exactly where you want it to. Countersteering is exactly that: turning the bars opposite to the direction you want to go. In a car or on an ATV or trike, the action is intuitive: turn right to go right, turn left to go left. But on a bicycle or motorcycle, the action is opposite: turn right to go left, turn left to go right. Mind you, because we've all spent years riding bicycles, this action is just as intuitive for most people; actually understanding what you are doing and consciously using the technique, however, will help you to get the most benefit out of it.

For a motorcycle to turn, it has to be leaned on its side in the direction of the turn. What we are doing when we countersteer is to force the bike over on its side, where physics, gravity, and the tires take over and do their jobs. There are two components to countersteering; the first is *gyroscopic precession*. If we think of the front wheel and tire as a big gyroscope, when we turn the bars to the right, precession forces the top of the wheel to fall to the left, and vice versa.

The second component is the *imbalance* created by steering the front wheel out from under the bike. If you turn the bars to the right at any amount of speed, the bike wants to keep on going straight, and literally falls over to the left—just like an ATV or a car will roll over to the left if you turn to the right too hard. This is why you see the occasional picture of riders exiting a corner, or in the middle of a chicane, with the wheel cocked in the opposite direction of the turn. The rider is trying so hard to turn the bike using countersteering that the front wheel is losing traction and tucking. Almost all of the effort in countersteering is coming from your arms pushing and pulling on the handlebars, and it takes exponentially more effort and strength to turn the bike at higher speeds. In a slow chicane, it's relatively easy to turn the bike from side to side, but in faster chicanes, like those on the short course at Silverstone, it can be so physical that you really have to manhandle the bike to get it through.

This is the first chapter in the book where the setup of your bike can affect what's happening. Here, how wide you have your clip-ons set, or how wide a handlebar you've got on your bike, can really make a difference as to how your bike steers. I used to have my bars open a little bit; it's a rider thing, but if you've got your bars open, it does give you a bit more leverage. In pictures of me on the bike, however, you can always see that I've only got half my hand on the bar. I've got my hand on the very outside of the handlebar, sometimes with my last two fingers not even on the bar, so I can get that extra leverage. I could have had wider bars, but I'd have probably just put my hands out even wider, which would affect other things. Having my bars open just that amount gives me the extra leverage I need, but also stops my hands from going too far out.

You can also change your bike's geometry set-

tings to make the steering easier, but with this, you sacrifice stability. Reducing the trail makes the steering lighter, and you can change this by lowering the front of the bike, raising the rear, decreasing the rake (as you can on some Ducati models), or increasing the offset—which you can do with adjustable triple clamps.

When I first started with Ducati in England, I almost always rode the bike with the 24.5-degree head-angle setting and 30mm of offset in the triple clamps. When I went to America and worked with Ernesto Marinelli on the Vance & Hines team, we used 23.5 degrees and 27mm or thereabouts—steeper rake, but more trail. And when I went to the factory team, we changed to 23.5 degrees and 26mm—even more trail. Then I left it like that for years, even when I went back to the superbike after riding MotoGP.

A rake of 23.5 degrees is quite steep, and you couldn't ride that setting with the offset way out for less trail. The steering would be so light that you'd be able to turn it with one finger, but the bike would just be so unstable, causing it to shake. Eventually we ended up with the offset as far in as 25mm, but that started to make the bike too hard to turn. At my regular setting, you had to put quite a bit of input into it, but the bike would turn in and you would always hit the spot. It just held its line so well. You had to

get it right; otherwise, you'd miss the apex a little bit.

A lot of guys didn't like that setup, but I liked it because it was so physical; I liked to have to put in a lot of effort to get the feedback and accuracy I wanted. Many riders prefer a more pointy setup, but mine was always lazy, like a chopper—always high in the front—which also increases trail.

As I mentioned earlier in the chapter, countersteering is the most effective way to turn your bike, and is responsible for the bulk of the steering. But at a certain level you will have to use your body to physically lean the bike, to help put it into the turn or to change direction. You can sit still on the bike and just turn the handlebars, but when you throw your bike from one side to the other, that really helps get it over. This means pushing on the footpegs with your feet, into the tank with your knees, and into the footpeg hangers with the insides of your feet—whatever you can use to help you physically move the bike underneath you from side to side.

In the top levels of racing, the riders weigh anywhere from 60 kilograms to 80 kilograms (130 to 175 pounds), and that is a huge portion of the

Setting your clip-ons wider than normal can give you more leverage for easier steering. I always had my bars open a bit on the race bikes, and I also kept my hands right at the ends of the bars—sometimes even with a couple of fingers over the edge, as you can see here.

(COURTESY OF DUCATI)

total weight of bike and rider. Compared to changing the rake or offset a small amount, your weight on the bike can make the biggest difference—not just for steering, but also for braking, accelerating, and almost everything else that we'll cover from this chapter onward. This is the biggest difference between a car and a motorcycle. When you're in the driver's seat and strapped in, you're stuck there. When a car is good, the driver can do the lap time, and both teammates are always quick. But when you've got two bikes the same, that doesn't mean that both riders' lap times will be good. A particular setup may work for one person, but it's not going to work for the next guy.

This is the case even in—well, you could say *especially* in—MotoGP. When Loris Capirossi and I used to both ride for Ducati in MotoGP, Loris used light fork springs, but the damping in his forks was incredibly hard. I'd use heavy fork springs and much softer damping, and there was no way I could ride his bike; it just felt way too stiff to me, and I was not comfortable with that at all. How much you hang off the bike, how much you lean forward or back, where you sit on the seat—it all affects how your bike works. Your weight on the bike, and how you move that weight around when trying to lean the bike from side to side, can have a huge influence

on how quickly and how accurately you can steer into a corner. (We'll get into more detail about body position in Chapter 6.)

Accurate steering calls for a definite reference point—a marker at the end of the straight where you initiate the turn into the corner, or a marker in the middle of a chicane where you transition from one side to the other. If you're doing everything right and pushing everything to the limit, it will take your maximum effort to turn the bike in and make the apex of the corner. A huge part of this transition also involves smoothly releasing the brakes as the bike is turned in, or *trail braking*, and we will discuss this at length in the next chapter. When you're on proper race pace, once you've begun that initial steering input, you're already committed to how you're going to do the corner. Ideally, you use your maximum input with your arms and your body to get the bike over on its side, smoothly reducing that input when the bike gets to maximum lean near the apex of the corner.

Some bikes, depending on their setup, don't want to change their line in the middle of the corner. When you've got more offset or less rake for quicker steering, you've got to put a lot less input into the bars to make a change in the middle of the corner. I always had my bikes set up with slower steering,

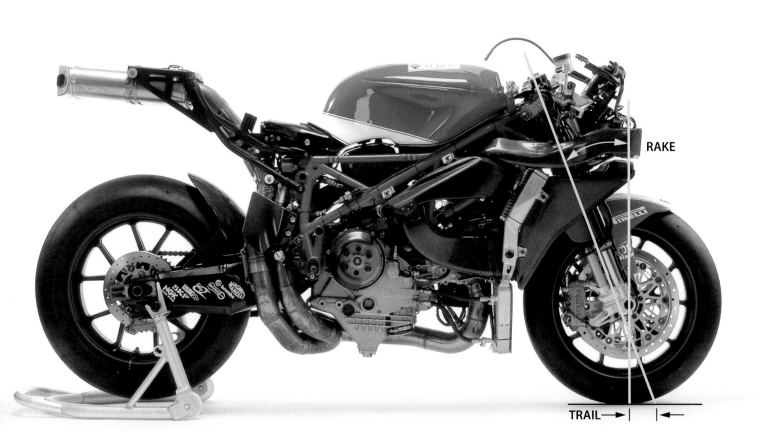

RAKE

TRAIL →| |←

Having a turn-in reference point, where you begin your arc into the corner, will help you to keep a consistent line into the corner. Here you want to smoothly release the brakes and lean the bike over in one fluid motion, right to maximum lean. **(COURTESY OF DUCATI)**

LEFT: Another way to decrease trail to make steering easier is to raise the rear end of the bike. On many Ducati models, this is easily accomplished using the adjuster in the linkage rod. **(COURTESY OF DUCATI)**

BELOW: If you do everything right steering into the corner, you will end up at full lean right at the apex of the turn. The goal is to not have to make any mid-corner corrections to your line or lean angle. If you do have to make a correction, however, use very light counter-steering on the bars rather than moving your body about on the bike. **(COURTESY OF DUCATI)**

and while the bike was always stable, I had to get that steering input right, because the bike was on a set line. I couldn't make any corrections in the corner because I was already at maximum everything. Once you get to that point in your riding, and you're able to accurately put the bike into the apex with maximum steering input, you can approach the corner differently to change your line, but once you're into the turn, you've already decided the line that you're going to take in that corner.

In an ideal world, you would not have to make any mid-corner corrections or change your lean angle in the middle of a turn; however, less-experienced track riders will find that they will need to make the occasional steering input in the middle of the corner to account for slightly more or less entry speed, or an earlier or later turn-in point. And street riders need to constantly make those corrections on an unfamiliar road, or to account for debris on the surface. In these cases you should use very light and minimal inputs into the bars to change your line using countersteering. At maximum lean, a countersteering input directly steers the front wheel and upsets the chassis much less than moving your body around on the bike does.

Exiting a turn is just the opposite of entering: You will have to countersteer or use your body to physically lift the bike up from full lean. And just as you need a marker where you begin your turn into the corner, having a reference point to aim for at the edge of the track on the exit will help. In general, your steering inputs at the exit of the corner do not have to be as aggressive as those on the entrance, but there are times when you will have to pull the bike up quite forcefully to get ready for the next corner; for example, when two corners are almost close enough together to be considered a chicane. This is where you can really see riders countersteering as they exit a turn. They are turning the bars so hard to lift the bike up that it steers the front wheel out from under the bike, in the same direction as the turn. Just as the brakes must be gradually released as you arc into a corner, the throttle must be gradually applied as you straighten the bike up and exit a turn. This can have a big effect on how your bike behaves coming out of a corner, especially if you're on a heavy, powerful superbike. We will address throttle control at length in Chapter 7.

CHAPTER 5

Braking

Races are won and lost on the brakes. Many times in the history of our sport, races have been decided by a last-lap, last-corner braking pass. It's a very important skill to have, even though super hard and late braking on its own doesn't improve the lap time by much.

On tracks with long straights and big, long braking zones, there's always plenty of room (and time) for good passing and braking maneuvers. When I raced in the United States with Vance & Hines at Daytona in 2000, Nicky Hayden, Mat Mladin, and I did a lot of passing: off of the tri-oval into turn 1, into the two horseshoes, and into the chicane. (The last lap at that track is always interesting for braking, as nobody wants to lead out of the chicane.)

At Daytona, or at a place like Monza, there are many times where you're just on and off your brake, as you can't find the limit every time and get it perfect. You might be 15 meters (or about 50 feet) behind

the rider in front of you when you start braking, but there's the draft to consider, your drive out of the last corner, and so many other variables. And sometimes, even if you could pass the other rider, you don't always want to; you're not always going mad on the brakes.

Being proficient on the brakes is a necessary skill to have in your toolbox, especially when it comes to race craft. And street riders will definitely want to have their braking technique down solid, as it's what most often gets you out of a dangerous situation. Braking well is not just about squeezing the lever or stomping on the pedal as hard as you can; it may have been at one time, but motorcycle brakes are so strong now that you can lock the front wheel with just one finger. How quickly you can apply the brakes and get to maximum deceleration, and how smoothly you release the brakes going into a corner, are just as important as how hard you can brake in the middle of the braking zone.

A lot of riders just don't know how hard a motorcycle can decelerate. Quite often it takes a ride on the back of the two-seater for people to realize the bike can go into a corner as hard as it does. Many riders don't use the front brake enough, but on motorcycles, most of the braking is done with the front brake. I always use the rear brake as well, and I'll address that later in the chapter, but the rear brake is not going to do very much as far as slowing you down.

Hard braking is not a skill you can expect to master in one session, or one day. It's something you'll have to work on constantly, and it does take a bit of time. There are three parts to consider: The first is the *bulk of the braking zone,* where you are applying the brakes for maximum stopping power. The second is the *initial application,* and getting smoothly and quickly to maximum braking. And the third is gently releasing the brakes as you tip into the corner—*trail braking.*

Before you can work on the initial application or trail braking, it's important to be comfortable with braking as hard as you can and generating the maximum stopping force. This is something best practiced at the track, in a long braking zone where you have plenty of time to get to your maximum braking, and experiment from there. Ideally, you should practice at a corner where there is a lot of runoff, preferably paved, so that you've got an escape route should something go wrong.

Maximum braking is not a matter of pulling on the lever as hard as you can; the limitations stem from the tires locking up and losing traction, or the rear

tire coming off the ground. Check the data graph from Phillip Island in the introduction, and you'll see that brake pressure is never steady and almost always changing as I'm on the brakes. You definitely want to try and have both wheels stay on the ground, and you'll know you're reaching one limit when the back wheel is either hopping or weaving. From the front, it's all feel. As the front tire nears locking up, it may howl or make a skidding noise, and you'll feel it start to squirm around. Bumps can really affect how the front tire behaves under braking, and you'll have to modulate the brake lever over any rough portions of the track.

When you're on the brakes, there's so much weight on your arms and shoulders. We used to put grip tape or something similar on the gas tank, and wipe the seat of the bike and the back of my leathers with contact cleaner so that I could hang on with my legs as much as possible. You want everything on your legs to grip so that you can keep your arms slightly bent at the elbows, taking as much weight off your upper body as you can. You should definitely sit up when you put the brake on so that your body catches some wind; that helps as well. A lot of riders stay tucked down and only come up a tiny bit when they're on the brake, but you want to be quite upright to catch a bit of wind. Because the back tire

RIGHT: Here you can see how much you can combine braking and turning to trail-brake into a corner. A lot of what goes into being able to do this is comfort and confidence, and you will definitely have to work up to this in small increments. **(COURTESY OF DUCATI)**

BELOW: When we had telemetry on the race bikes, the guys would say I was wasting power because I was using the rear brake on corner exits. But I'd be doing that and I'd still have the throttle on. If I didn't have the rear brake on, I'd just be using less throttle. **(COURTESY OF DUCATI)**

RIGHT: Using a zip tie on your front fork tube will show how much travel you are using when braking. While small changes in setup may not really affect your braking, you definitely do not want the forks bottoming out. **(ANDREW TREVITT)**

will be coming off the ground, you should also try to push yourself back in the seat to load the rear tire as much as you can. Add all of this to trying to keep the weight off your arms, and things can get tricky; you have to manage by gripping your legs on the tank and holding your upper body steady with your abdominal muscles.

Hard braking is something you'll have to work up to in relatively small increments. Begin your braking at the same point each time, gradually applying the brakes as you would normally; when you get to what you think is your maximum braking, apply a bit more force on the lever. Pay attention to the feedback you get from the front and rear tires, and release the lever slightly if there's a problem. If you're able to brake harder and find yourself with room to spare at the corner, only then should you begin your braking at a later point the next time. Working the other way—simply braking later to force yourself to brake harder to make the corner—brings panic into play, and doesn't allow you to concentrate on what you're actually doing.

How many fingers you use on the lever can make a big difference in braking and steering control, as well as affecting how smoothly and quickly you're able to go from throttle to brake at the end of the straight, and again from brake to throttle in the corner. Using one or two fingers gives you a better grip on the handlebar and more control for steering while braking; using more fingers, however, gives you more power and control to work the front brake. A lot of it is style and how comfortable you feel. Some riders use the middle two fingers, some riders use three, and some riders use all four. I use the first two fingers on the front brake, but Valentino Rossi uses his whole hand. I don't think he does it for a particular reason; I think it's just part of his style. It certainly doesn't slow him up, because he's pretty good . . . .

You will need a good braking system if you're using two fingers, as you don't want the lever coming too close to the bar and trapping the other two fingers. Most bikes now have really strong brakes and it's not a problem, and many race bikes have an adjuster to change the lever position during a race. There was a time where the adjuster on my front brake broke during a race, and the lever started to hit my fingers on the bar; I had to use my whole hand on the brakes. The feeling while I was braking was okay, but I really struggled with coming off the brakes and back onto the throttle. I didn't feel as much in control as I do when I use two fingers.

Once you're comfortable that you are braking at your maximum, it's time to work on the initial application of the brakes. We will discuss reference points in detail in Chapter 8, but of course you will need a braking marker. Most tracks have numbered boards, cones, or something similar leading up to each corner. A lot of where you begin your braking depends on the prior corner, and how good a job you did on the exit. You've got to take that into account when you brake at the next corner, as you could be going a few kilometers per hour faster or slower. It's just like the start of a race: The braking mark for the first corner will be much later because you're starting from a standstill in the middle of the straight.

Many riders cheat themselves at the braking marker by letting off the throttle slowly and putting their fingers on the brake well beforehand, finally grabbing the lever at their marker board. The time it takes to do this can make a big difference. Some people use the marker board as a reference point to hold the throttle open, rather than as a point to start braking, and this helps to speed that transition from open throttle to braking. You want to close the throttle and get your fingers on the lever and the brakes applied as quickly as you can. (Note in the data graph shown in the introduction how

the throttle position trace drops quickly from full throttle to zero at the end of most straights.) Here's one way of looking at it: If you can reduce the time that this transition takes by a quarter of a second, which is a pretty reasonable goal, you'll be able to move your braking marker by almost 15 meters (49 feet) when braking into a 200 kph (125 mph) corner. You can outbrake a lot of people at the track in that much distance, and on the street you will have that much more of a safety cushion should you have to stop quickly.

The temptation when you apply the brakes is to grab them as forcefully as you can to get to maximum deceleration right away. That may work in a car, but on a bike you have to work your way in, to allow the front suspension to compress and the weight to transfer onto the front tire. If you grab too much brake right away—before you have that weight transfer—the front tire will lock up, and that can lead to a crash. It takes even an expert-level rider close to a full second to take all that into account and get from full throttle to maximum braking. Still, you want to get to your maximum as quickly as you can after that initial application, because you are covering a lot of distance at speed. The earlier in the braking zone that you can scrub that speed off, the shorter your stopping distance will be.

At the far end of the braking zone, the entry to the corner, you will have to gradually release the brakes as you lean the bike into the corner. Most people don't realize how late—and how much—you can brake when the bike is on its side, arcing into a corner. And when you enter the turn like that, it's easier to steer the bike, as the front suspension is compressed, changing the geometry. In many chicanes, when you are on the brakes right into the first part of the corner, you can just flip the bike onto its side. Anywhere that you're off the gas and on the brake, you've already got the front a little bit loaded, and it makes changing direction easier.

Most of the top riders—me included—brake right into the corner with the bike leaned over. When you can do that and have a great feel for the tire while the bike's on its side, that's often where you find the last bit of speed that separates the fast riders from the really fast riders. Finding that bit of feeling is the hardest thing, and something you will have to steadily and carefully work up to. Realistically, as the bike's tipping in, you should be getting lighter on the brake, and then the lever should be released at the apex of the corner. Again, this is not something to work on simply by braking later and hoping for the best when you get to the corner and have to turn in on the brakes. Rather, brake at the same point, but keep the brakes on a bit longer, as you tip the bike in. Once you get the feel for what's happening and are comfortable with a certain level of trail braking, then you can move your braking marker closer to the corner. Keep working in steps, adding more braking with increased lean angle in increments.

How much you can trail-brake does depend on your setup, and on your bike. Sometimes you've simply got to use the brake and hold it on to get the bike to tip in as quickly as you'd like, depending on your forks or your setup. It can be difficult to get the confidence and feeling necessary to do that, but once you find something that works, you can really use it to your advantage.

In the old days with Michelin, the front tires needed to be forced hard; they didn't work until they were really loaded. It was difficult to get comfortable and do that. It was a big workup to get there, and a big confidence thing, but once I got there, I could do it regularly. In the early 2000s, they had so many different compounds and carcasses, you could be fine on one tire, but then you could put on another tire and be going two seconds a lap slower, without any feel for it at all. Colin Edwards and I used to use totally different front tires; the rubber would be similar, but the carcass would be so different.

Other aspects of setup can be just as important when it comes to getting that feel and confidence in the front end. I used to change lots of settings in the early days, but in the end, once you've got a really good base setup on your bike, something you really believe in and you know works, minor adjustments—1 or 2 millimeters more preload, a slightly stiffer or softer spring, more or less oil—all you're doing is giving yourself that confidence and feeling for braking as hard as you can. The bike will probably be able to do it anyway, but if you can make it a bit more comfortable and you like the action that the bike is doing, it will help to give you the confidence.

t all goes back to comfort and the example I used in the last chapter, about setup. Loris Capirossi and I used completely different fork setups on the Ducati MotoGP bike—there was no way I could ride his bike—but he could brake just as hard and deep into the corner as I could with my setup. And Colin and I were quite often evenly matched under braking, even with those very different front tires we were using.

When it comes to using the rear brake, there are many different viewpoints. Some people use the rear brake all the time, while others never touch it on the track. I use the rear brake everywhere, especially on the entry into the corner, to help stabilize the rear end of the bike. I always used a foot brake, rather than a hand lever on the left clip-on, like some riders do, and I use the rear brake right from the first application of the front brake—sometimes even earlier. In some situations, I'd just touch the rear brake before I'd roll off the gas, and that would help to settle the bike a little bit.

Using the foot brake lets me use the rear brake all the way into the apex in a left-hand corner, but only on the initial braking in a straight line for a right-hand corner. As soon as you start to bend the bike over into a right-hand corner, you've got to move your foot up away from the lever and into position, which is with the ball of your foot on the footpeg. So from there you're relying on engine braking to slow the rear wheel down and keep things in line. Then it depends on how you have adjusted the fueling and slipper clutch settings (if you can change them), to get enough engine braking to have the feeling you want.

At Mugello, for example, braking for the long last corner is a place where I used to use a lot of rear brake, even with the bike totally leaned over. It's a double-apex, left-hand turn and slightly downhill, and by the time you hit the first apex, that's where

The last corner at Mugello is a tricky, downhill, third-gear turn with two apexes. You've got to have good feeling on the brakes to go quick here. I am off the front brake by the first apex, and then I run it out to the middle of the track. From there, I can use the rear brake to close up my line to make the second apex. **(GOLD & GOOSE)**

you're off the front brake. Then you run it out into the middle of the track a little. I'm not sure if that was helping the rear end to just hang out a little bit, to turn the bike, or just sitting the rear of the bike down, but it's there that I could close the corner a little bit with the rear brake if I had to; this would help me to find the correct line in the middle of the corner.

To be honest, when you've got the bike so far leaned over into a corner, you haven't got a lot of rear brake on because you simply can't use a lot. You can have your foot sitting there, but you're not actually going to be doing much with it. The rear brake is all from the initial application at the marker to where you first start to bend the bike in; there's hardly any rear brake beyond that stage. In left-hand corners I have my foot on the brake nearly the whole time, and as soon as I get on the gas, I have my foot on the brake at the same time. For me it's a safety thing; I use the rear brake to control wheelies on the exit. As with a lot of things, there is no right or wrong way when it comes to using the rear brake. But for me, the only time I *didn't* have my foot on the rear brake was in the middle of a right-hand corner.

Being confident in your braking will help tremendously when you ride on the street. In a dangerous situation, you want to be able to brake at your best without really thinking about it, so that you can con-centrate more on what's happening around you rather than on the braking itself. Ideally, you wouldn't get in a spot where you have to use your brakes heavily; this means keeping plenty of distance between you and the cars in front of you and watching carefully for potential hazards, so that when something *does* happen, you've got plenty of room to slow or stop.

On twisty roads, it's a good idea to use less trail braking than you would at the track, if any at all. Trail braking really loads the front end of the motorcycle, and if the pavement is at all slippery or bumpy, there's more of a chance of a crash. Because you aren't braking as heavily on the street as you would on the track, the rear brake is much more useful in many situations; it's especially handy to modulate your speed in long corners, rather than being on and off the throttle constantly.

Whether you ride on the street or track, braking is a very important skill. Experienced and inexperienced riders alike can benefit from being able to brake harder, getting on the brakes quicker and braking more with the bike leaned over into a corner. It's well worth regularly working on each aspect, both individually and combined.

CHAPTER 6:
Body Position

When the Hockenheimring in Germany was on the World Superbike calendar, it was the full course with four very long straights. I first went there in 2000, shortly after I was brought into the Ducati team to fill in for Carl Fogarty. During practice and qualifying I had a lot of trouble with setup; I couldn't even hold the throttle open on the first straight after the NordKurve, as the bike would just get into a weave. We tried a few things with the bike, but in the end it was the way I was sitting on the bike and where my feet, knees, and elbows were. My riding position was just upsetting the bike so much aerodynamically that it was making it unstable.

I ended up winning my first World Superbike race that weekend, but if I hadn't experimented with my body position and constantly moved around on the seat, trying to find a solution, it certainly would have been a different story. So many people, when they think of body position on a motorcycle,

> **OPPOSITE:** The bikes these days have all got a lot of power, so you have to use some of your body position to stop them from wheeling. **(COURTESY OF DUCATI)**

worry about being picture-perfect in the middle of the corner. There's so much more to it than that. Your body position interacts with how you've got the motorcycle set up; it can help you better muscle the bike around in a chicane, and it can even make a huge difference on a straightaway—as I found out at the Hockenheimring.

Body position is something that has a huge impact on the whole bike, and something you've got to experiment with and understand in order to get the most benefit from it. We've already covered some of the basics in previous chapters, and as I've mentioned, the most common mistake I see when riding with people is that they think they need to stay tucked down all the time in a racing position, even when they brake or are in the middle of a turn. While you do want to be tucked in on a straight, you want to sit up when you're braking in order to use your body for a windbreak, with your elbows almost locked to hold yourself upright. And in the middle of the corner, you want to be hanging off but in a nice, comfortable, and relaxed position that allows you to properly steer the bike and easily make any control inputs necessary. These are three distinctly different body positions; not only is it important to become familiar and comfortable with each of them, but it's also essential that you know how to smoothly transition among each of the three.

On a straight of almost any length, you want to get fully tucked in to make yourself as slippery as possible to the wind. This means putting your head and chest down on the tank to make yourself small behind the windscreen; you will most likely have to push yourself right back in the seat to make room. Your elbows should be in tight to the tank, tucked in front of your knees if there's enough room.

Another common thing I see on the track, especially with newer riders, is that they keep their heels on the pegs all the time. This causes problems in the corners for ground clearance, but even on the straight, you should have the balls of your feet on the pegs to help with aerodynamics. This is one thing I've always had trouble with myself. Davide Tardozzi would always mention it to me; sometimes I'd even see him on the pit wall, pointing at my feet. I've always ridden like Daffy Duck, with my feet sticking out, and I realize it's not very aerodynamic. I may have had the fastest bike in the paddock, but very rarely was I the fastest through the speed traps. Even in the wind tunnel, Neil Hodgson and Ruben Xaus were always much more aerodynamic than me, even though they are bigger.

A straight is also a good place to relax on the bike and catch your breath. You especially want to take the pressure off your arms and hands—not completely open them up and let go of the bars, but take some of the weight off them. Being light on the bars on a straight can also help with stability, especially when the track's bumpy. Holding on tight often makes a wobble worse once it starts. The natural tendency for people is to grip the bars as tight as they can, especially if the bike is not working exactly how they'd like it to work. They end up hanging on more than they should, and this can give you "arm pump."

I was lucky that this was never a really big issue for me, but sometimes I did get it. If I did, it would typically be at the start of the weekend, just because I was in a hurry to get going and wasn't relaxed on the bike. You can end up with sore arms for several days after a race if you get a bad case of arm pump, and some people struggle with it throughout their whole career. The faster bikes are more physical, and most people end up riding these eventually, so every bit of energy that you can save on the straight will help you in other areas, especially in a longer race.

As we covered in the previous chapter, you'll

I won my first World Superbike race at Hocken-heim in 2000, but it wouldn't have been possible if I hadn't been able to sort out my body position on the straights to make the bike more stable. At first the bike would weave so badly on the straight that I couldn't even hold the throttle open. You can see some of the trouble in this image from Brands Hatch that year: I was always sticking my toes out, and that was affecting the bike's aerodynamics. **(GOLD & GOOSE)**

need to sit up when braking so that the wind helps to slow you down. You'll most likely find yourself naturally moving forward on the seat early in the braking zone, but then you should try to push yourself back in the seat to transfer as much weight to the back as you can, to stop the rear tire from lifting. You do want at least some bend in your elbows, as this makes it easier to steer the bike; if your elbows are completely locked, you can't turn the bars without rotating your whole upper body. This requires you to hold yourself up using a lot of abdominal muscles and squeezing the tank with your knees.

On the bigger bikes, like the Superbikes and GP machines, there is so much force on the brakes that sometimes you've got to nearly lock your elbows. And then you start looking for those little extra things to make it easier—grip tape on the tank, scuffed-up leathers, and so on. A couple of times, when I had a slippery seat or new leathers, I'd have to come in straightaway and have someone drag me across the ground to scrape up my leathers, or put contact cleaner on the seat so my legs wouldn't slip. Anything to save my arms and shoulders for braking.

In a corner, you obviously want to move your body to the inside of the turn so that you can keep the bike as upright as possible for more traction. Some riders don't hang off very much, while you'll see others hanging way off, with their heads low and their elbows on the ground. When you get going quickly on the race track, you'll have to hang off at least a certain amount in order to be safe on the corner exits; less-experienced riders usually think they are hanging off a lot more than they actually are, and I have to tell them to exaggerate it, especially as they go faster. However, if you hang off too much, you won't be able to steer and control the bike as much as you may need to.

For me, hanging way off feels busy and doesn't make sense with the way I like to have my setup. I've always had my bikes with lazy steering, and I like to be more physical with them; that means not hanging off excessively so that I can really force the bars around when I transition from side to side.

When you get your body off to the side of the bike, it's important to bring your whole body over and not just get your butt off the seat. Ideally, your upper body stays parallel to the centerline of the bike, with your head off the side of the bike just as much. Remember: The whole idea is to keep the bike as upright as you can, so if your upper body is not over the centerline, it's not helping in that respect. Your head should be level with the ground so that your eyes are parallel with the horizon; this can help to keep you from getting dizzy.

Some riders like to pivot around the back of the tank—like Mick Doohan, for example—while others keep their hips square with the bike. I usually keep my hips square, but I think it depends a lot on the setting, or type of bike, as sometimes I find myself riding with more of a pivoted style. How you position your hips is really a matter of personal comfort—whatever lets you easily keep your upper body in line with the bike. There's a lot of variance in how a person's pelvis and hip sockets are actually formed and put together, and for some people, their hips just move easier in a certain way.

As I touched on earlier, how you position your feet on the pegs is also important. In a corner, the ball of your inside foot should be on the peg so that you've got as much ground clearance as possible. On the outside, your heel should be on the peg, right in the cutout portion of your boot. This lets you reach the rear brake or shifter if you need to, and it also allows you to turn your foot outward to open up your leg and hip, in turn making it easier to hang off the inside of the bike. As you can imagine, that means a lot of moving around on the pegs when you go from braking to turning, and from side to side in a chicane.

When you're moving around on your bike, remember that your body weight is a huge portion of the overall weight, and any sudden movements can easily upset the chassis. For example, when you transition from braking to turning, you don't want to jump off the side of the bike right when you tip into the corner.

For me, in a braking zone the bike is usually completely upright, and I have my body straight as I concentrate on braking. I like to slide off to the side just as I start to get a little bit into the turn, sometimes slightly before I tip in. If you get off to the side too early, you can't hold on strongly enough for braking; too late, and you'll unsettle the bike as it gets close to maximum lean. The same thing applies at the exit: You want to keep your body off the side of the bike until the bike is upright, then smoothly slide yourself back into the center of the seat and get into your tuck for the straight. There's no rush to get back to the centerline, and you definitely don't want to upset the chassis right when you are searching for every last bit of traction. The bikes these days have all got a lot of power, and you have to use your body position to stop them wheelying; slide your butt forward on the seat and lean your head and chest as far forward as possible under acceleration.

When to move your body to change direction in the middle of a chicane is not so clear. I try to make it so that as I lean the bike from one side to the other,

RIGHT: Just as I talked about in the previous chapter, on a long and twisty mountain road you will wear yourself out within a few miles if you hang off in every turn and move around on the bike a lot. Here, it's more about comfort and lasting all day, so a better option is to remain centered and steer more with your arms rather than muscling the bike about. **(COURTESY OF DUCATI)**

BELOW RIGHT: You don't want your feet to be slipping off the pegs. My footpegs were always filed to points and would destroy a set of boots in one weekend; they'd be finished, because the last thing I wanted was my feet sliding around. **(COURTESY OF DUCATI)**

ABOVE: A lot of people run their handlebars a lot lower than I do, but I thought the lower you've got your handlebars, the more weight you're putting on your wrists and shoulders. Because I had the bike setup quite lazy and had to be physical with the steering, the higher handlebars were more comfortable for me. **(COURTESY OF DUCATI)**

my body is coming across the bike and I'm pulling on the bars at the same time. This lets me use the momentum of my body to physically lift the bike and change direction quickly. So many people said I used to be able to change direction quickly in places such as Ascari at Monza, or other fast chicanes where it's really hard to get the bike from side to side. I was really physical with it. I would get across using my body, pulling on the handlebar to help get the bike back under me—sometimes hard enough to lift the front wheel off the ground. Just as I use my legs and torso to keep the weight off my arms when braking or in a turn, I also use those muscles to move my body across the bike as fast as possible, while using less weight on my arms to free them up for actually steering the motorcycle.

How you position your hand and foot controls can make a big difference, not only to how comfortable you are on the bike, but also how easily you can move around on it to use your weight. For example, a lot of MotoGP riders who move into Superbike use clip-ons with a lot of angle—16.5 or 17 degrees. I think that's because most of them came from riding in the 125 and 250 classes, and they were used to it.

I ran that for a while when I rode in MotoGP but I didn't like it; I thought the lower bars put more weight on my shoulders and wrists. I liked the bars

high, because I had to be very physical with the lazy way I had my bike set up, and the higher they were, the more comfortable I was. When I went back to MotoGP and won the race at Valencia in 2006, we took my handlebars and forks out of the Superbike and put them straight on the MotoGP bike. So I ran my usual bars with 6.5-degree angle, and the bike was perfect for me.

As far as footpeg height, you will most likely have to sacrifice at least a bit of comfort for ground clearance. One thing to remember, though, is that with higher pegs, it's easier to move your weight around; you're more like a jockey on a horse, and

OPPOSITE: Compare my body position (top) to Noriyuki Haga's. They are definitely different, but our bikes are also set up very differently. On the one hand, we each have our own style to take advantage of the way we like to have the bike set up; and on the other hand, we set up the bike so it works best with the style and body position with which we are the most comfortable. **(HAGA IMAGE COURTESY OF DUCATI, BAYLISS IMAGE BY GOLD & GOOSE)**

can easily get your butt off the seat. The Panigale has more legroom than previous Ducatis, and when we first started testing it, I was nowhere near as sore in the hips and hip flexors as I used to be on the old bike. But as soon as we got going we had to move the footpegs up for ground clearance. Straightaway that made the lap times better, and not only because of the better ground clearance; having them higher also made it a lot easier for me to move around on the bike.

How you use your weight and where you place it can affect how your bike is set up. Just moving your clip-ons forward or back by 10mm, or putting some foam at the rear of the tank or on the seat, can make a big difference in where your weight is and how you have the suspension as a result. If we compare my style to Noriyuki Haga's, for example, his body and head are all in line and his body is straight, but all at more of an angle than I am. When I look at Nori's bike, he has the bars mounted close to the forks and not very wide, whereas I used to have them about an inch further forward and out wider. To me, that means Nori's bike must be set to turn easily, and his bike

did always seem to look high on the back and a bit more nervous.

With my bikes all lazy-steering and me having to be more physical, leaning off the bike as far as Nori does wouldn't make sense for my style. But at the same time, I don't think I would have liked to have ridden the bike the way he has it set up. The relationship between setup and body position is a two-way street: Both Nori and I set up our bikes to suit our individual styles. But we have those particular styles and body positions because that's what works with the way we've each set up our bikes.

As with most aspects of riding a motorcycle, there is no clear right or wrong when it comes to body position; to a certain point, of course. Work toward being comfortable on the bike, but don't be afraid to move outside your comfort zone and experiment with changes to your body position, as well as changes to your controls and settings, to better suit your own style.

CHAPTER 7:
Throttle Control

With all the advancements in electronic rider aids over the last few years—traction control, wheelie control, auto blip, quick shifters, and so on—it may seem like throttle control is becoming a lost art. But until you're riding for a factory team where they can really work the electronics around you, traction control can really slow you down more than help you go faster. More and more racing series are heading toward spec ECUs or limits on the electronics, in which case throttle control will be more important than ever. And even though traction control gets better every year, I still like it off sometimes, just to have a little bit of fun!

In Chapter 5, we talked about riders who have good front-tire feel when the bike is on its side under braking, and how that separates the good riders from

OPPOSITE: Even though the advancement of traction control and other rider aids is reducing the importance of throttle control, it is still a valuable skill to have. Riders who have a good feel for rear tire traction and throttle control at partial openings often have an advantage over their competitors, even in series with unrestricted electronics. (COURTESY OF DUCATI)

the great ones. Likewise, it's that feel for rear-tire traction on acceleration out of a corner that can make the difference between riders, and that takes good throttle control. While accelerating out of a corner is the most important aspect of throttle control, we'll also talk about upshifting, downshifting, and blipping the throttle in this chapter, and some circumstances where the throttle is rolled off rather than closed quickly.

Upshifting may seem like an easy task, and with more bikes coming standard with a quick shifter, you don't have to worry so much about it. But it's still worth knowing how to do it well manually in case you have a problem with the quick shifter—and that's something that applies to any of the electronic aids. I like to use the reverse pattern for shifting, or what I will call the "proper" shift—up for first gear and down for the rest. When you push the gear lever down to shift, you can make it more precise and quicker than with a standard shift pattern. This way also lets you make a shift when you're leaned over in a left-hand turn if you have to; with a standard shift, you can't always get your foot under the lever.

I used the standard method for a very long time, until I got a ride at the Suzuka 8 Hours with Peter

Goddard. He made me change to the proper way because I was going to partner him for the race. I felt so uncomfortable at first, and it took me a long time to get used to it; I really thought it was going to interfere with the way I was riding. I eventually got used to it. If you race or do a lot of track days, it's good to get your head around doing the race pattern.

On any straight, you should use full throttle and shift at redline to make the most of your engine's power. Surprisingly, a great number of people at the track don't use full throttle or maximum rpm on the straights. To make an upshift, if you don't have a quick shifter, you still don't have to use the clutch, and you don't have to fully close the throttle. All you need to do is roll the throttle off a fraction—just enough to unload the transmission—and select the next gear. If your timing is right, and you do it with just the slightest of movements, you can do it nearly as fast as a quick shifter. It's all about the connection between your wrist and your foot, and when you get the timing right, you hardly even back the throttle off.

There are some times when you don't want to, or will be unable to, shift at maximum rpm. Most often, it's on the exit of a left-hand corner where you can't get your foot to the gear lever. Here you can shift before redline, a "short shift." At Misano, on the old track when it ran counterclockwise, the series of long lefts was one of my favorite sections in the championship. The first corner was a first-gear corner; you'd come out of there and let the bike rev pretty hard in first. Then you'd select second and short-shift to third, and tip the bike straight back into the next left. If you'd left it in second, the bike was on its side, so you couldn't get to the gear lever. If you're racing using street-pattern shifting and the bike's on its side, it's even more difficult. The short shift here would help to get the bike settled to go into that left-hander.

There are also times when you are leaned over for a long time and don't necessarily want full power, or to upset the chassis by making a shift while leaned over. For example, exiting MG corner at Phillip Island, you give it as much throttle as you can, and then as the bike's going from the right to the left, you catch two gears right away. Then you have a long corner where the bike is on its side; if you don't make the shift early, you have to go from second to third with the bike completely on its side, where the slightest movement can upset it. It's a long corner, and you don't need a lot of acceleration, so you can be comfortable hanging off the bike and just getting all the drive you can find.

As I discussed in Chapter 5, at the end of the straight you usually want to close the throttle and

get on the brakes as quickly as you can. If the corner speed is only slightly less than the speed you are carrying at the end of the straight, or if the corner is fast enough that you are still accelerating as you turn in, it may be better to roll off the throttle rather than close it abruptly. A good example of this is turn 1 at Laguna Seca, which is the kink going over the hill on the front straight. Here, you're turning in on full throttle, but you have to roll off a little because the bike gets so light over the top. You don't even completely close the throttle; it's only a slight roll-off.

Another example is the Hayshed at Phillip Island, a fourth-gear corner. Again, you are going into the corner flat out, but you have to roll off—just enough to let the front settle over the bumps and the dip in the corner—and then get back on the throttle. You can see this at about the 2,800-foot mark on the Phillip Island data graph in the introduction. In both of these corners, it's the same situation: You only roll off to let the bike turn in and get a bit of grip before you can open the throttle again to help you change direction.

All through my career I never used the clutch on downshifts, but I always blipped the throttle with each one. When I left the pit box for a session, I didn't touch the clutch again until I came back in and put the bike in neutral. The system we had worked so well that I never had to worry about using the clutch and feeding it into the corner to make it smooth. On a production bike, such as the two-seater I have, I sometimes use the clutch to be a bit nicer to it and (hopefully) make it last a bit longer, although I've never had problems. Some riders like to take advantage of the electronics and slipper clutches to use the clutch without blipping the throttle, but I just hate the sound of a bike that hasn't had the throttle blipped. It sounds very cruel to the gearbox, and you're asking for compression lockup; that can really unsettle the chassis into a corner, and even lead to a highside. Unless you're riding in MotoGP or a class where the electronics are really good, I think it's a must to blip the throttle.

On bikes without a slipper clutch, you will definitely have to both use the clutch and blip the throttle for a smooth downshift. In any case, the idea is to match the engine rpm to the road speed with each downshift, so that when you complete the shift and release the clutch, there is no lurch as the wheel tries to catch up with the engine. When you brake and downshift at the end of a straight, the correct number of downshifts will need to be completed so that you are in the right gear just before you turn into the corner.

The danger of making a downshift too early is that the engine could over-rev when you let the clutch out, causing some damage. Too late, and you will be in too low of a gear for the corner, or you will have to downshift while turning—not a good mix. If you get the timing right, so that the engine revs perfectly match the road speed each time you engage a gear, it will be a smooth and quick shift, even without using the clutch. Almost always, you will be braking hard and having to manage the throttle when downshifting, and this is one of the major reasons to use just two fingers on the front brake—so that you can blip the throttle without affecting your braking.

I mentioned in Chapter 1 how critical the first application of the throttle is once you're in the corner, and how it should be as smooth as possible. Some of that is the mapping of the bike and the characteristics of the engine, but a large part of it is how smooth and precise you are with the throttle. The smoother you are on the throttle, the less you will unsettle the chassis; in turn, you will be able to open the throttle earlier. In any corner, but especially the long sweepers, you definitely want to avoid opening and closing the throttle repeatedly, as this will really upset the bike; once the throttle is open for the first time at the apex, it should stay open from there. When you have the throttle open but are not fully on the gas, you have to keep everything very smooth in order to keep the chassis settled for maximum corner speed, and there's a lot of concentration required.

Once the throttle is open at the apex, how you exit the corner is dependent on your own style. Ernesto used to always say that if he compared me with Lorenzo Lanzi, we had our bikes set quite differently because of our riding styles. He thought that Lorenzo put the power on when the bike was still on its side, whereas I used to get the bike up and could get on the gas harder because the bike was upright. I believe that you don't change a person's style; you just set the bike to work around it. That said, bikes

RIGHT: While it's best to close the throttle quickly at the end of most straights, there are some situations where smoothly rolling off the throttle is necessary. If you only need to scrub off enough speed to settle the front end of the bike, you may not even have to fully close the throttle. This is turn 1 at Laguna Seca, where you have to just slightly close the throttle going over the crest of the hill as the bike unloads. **(GOLD & GOOSE)**

LEFT: Throttle control is almost more important on the street than on the race track, as you spend much more time at partial throttle in this environment. Because there is less traction and it is constantly changing, having that feel for rear tire traction and good command of the throttle is crucial. **(COURTESY OF DUCATI)**

BELOW: On a smaller, less-powerful bike you can get away with accelerating on the side of the tire, but on the bigger bikes you will have to quickly lift the bike up from full lean, spending as little time as possible on the edge of the tire. **(COURTESY OF DUCATI)**

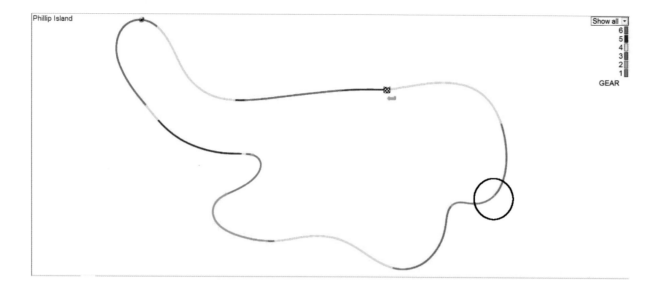

Phillip Island

Show all ▾

6
5
4
3
2
1
GEAR

are getting faster, the braking and accelerating, better, but they are still big bikes. The important thing is getting into the corner, turning, and getting out of there. If you ride around like you are on a 125, you are wasting too much time on the brakes and too much time getting on the gas. A 125 may be faster than a MotoGP bike or a superbike in the middle of the corner, but on the big bike, it's more important to get into the corner as fast as possible, turn, and get out.

It's important to understand that once you are at the exit of the corner and have the throttle open, you have to stand the bike upright before you can apply the gas to begin accelerating. If you miss the corner by even a little bit, and you're still trying to make the corner and open the throttle, it turns to rubbish. Everything has to be done properly and in order: turn in, open the throttle, start lifting, and apply the gas to accelerate. From the apex of the

OPPOSITE: Compare my style and Lorenzo Lanzi's style at the exit of this corner at Valencia. Ernesto always said we had different setups to work with our different styles. (COURTESY OF DUCATI)

ABOVE: This track map of Phillip Island was generated using data acquisition, and matches the data shown in the introduction. Here, the colors used for the map indicate which gear I am using. Note the short shift from first to third exiting MG corner, circled in black, as I turn the bike from right to left. (COURTESY OF DUCATI)

corner, you have to be lifting the bike all the way to the rumble strip at the exit, or where you have to change direction for the next corner.

On a bike with traction control, I still ride exactly the way I would on a bike without it; it's there to give you a hand on the corner exit rather than to do all the work for you. The throttle control should help to create a partnership between you and the bike, working together, rather than you just opening the throttle to the stop and relying on the bike. Traction control can definitely slow you down if you have the wrong setting, but that's not to say you can ride faster with it turned off. If you switched it right off, you would not be as fast, or as safe. A lot of the systems on the bikes now are so good, and they work so well with the rider's input, that it's difficult to tell just how much it's helping you. When I ride my standard S model with DTC at the track, I usually like to have the system set on level 2 of 8 (where 1 is the least intervention, and 8, the most). I don't want to feel it working too much and slowing the bike down, but I do want it to help save me from a highside.

We've been through the entire sequence for a regular corner: closing the throttle, braking, arcing from the outside to the apex on the brakes, letting off the brakes and setting the throttle, and finally, lifting the bike as you apply the throttle and accelerate. Some

chicanes, if the corners are similar and close together, are taken the same way: brake, turn into the first apex, and set the throttle. Then you pick up the throttle to a certain point, say one-third open, and turn the bike in the opposite direction, keeping that amount of throttle on to the second apex. Depending on the corner, you may have to open or close the throttle slightly, just to set the speed for the second part of the chicane. Once you're at the second apex, you are opening the throttle as per normal. There is only one example I can think of where you brake through an entire chicane, and that's at the Lausitzring. You go into a fast left, on the brakes and over the rumble strip; you go into the right; and then you're still braking as you tip it up and over to the left. There are not many corners like that.

If you don't open the throttle between the two corners of a chicane, and you pick up that tiny bit of speed, you will lose too much time. So many chicanes are like that, and require you to open the throttle so as not to lose any speed. As well, the bike turns faster from side to side when you've got the gas on. As soon as you pick up the throttle, the front extends, and it's helping you to get back over to the other side.

It's not as if you're going to full throttle, but rather just enough to help you get the bike from one side to the other. As the corners get farther and farther apart in a chicane, you will find that you need more throttle between them, and eventually they become two distinct corners. You will have to accelerate and then brake as you are moving the bike from one side to the other. The key is to get on the throttle to keep as much speed as you can between the two corners, even if it means just a short burst of throttle and a bit of braking between the two corners.

Even though more and more bikes are equipped as standard with good traction control and other electronics, many people would like it if there was no traction control in any of the racing series, just to see some really great racing where the throttle is completely in the riders' hands. If that's the case—and some series have already gone in that direction—then good throttle control will be more important than ever, as it's not easy managing a powerful bike without some electronic help. It's definitely worth taking advantage of the electronics if you have them and they aren't slowing you down, but know that at some point you will have to ride without the help; the more prepared you are, the better.

THE START

I've always had good starts through my career, and never had a jump start. To me it seems easy, but I see many people make simple mistakes and mess it up. In World Superbike and MotoGP, there is no green light to go; you've just got a red light. When it goes out, you leave. You want just one thing to concentrate on for the signal to go; pick one of the lights to go by, or if it's a flag-person, watch the tip of the flag for the first signs of movement. You should have both feet down so that you've got good balance, and know the bike's at 90 degrees. Sit as close to the fuel tank and lean as far forward as you can to get your weight on the front end. Even at world level I see so many people twisting the throttle and the revs going up and down, but if the revs are low when the light goes out, you've got to wait to get them back up again. Pick an engine speed for your "launch" rpm and hold it steady. Less-powerful bikes, such as a 125 GP bike or 600cc Supersport, will need lots of revs; bigger bikes need less. I'd never look at the tach on the superbike, but I'd hold the revs at five or six thousand; it wouldn't have to be revving hard for a strong start.

Motocross riders have a device to click the forks down and load the front end. You can do the same thing with a street bike by using the front brake and letting the clutch halfway out. You can lower the front by 20 to 25mm doing this, and then straightaway you have an advantage. When the lights go out, all you've got to do is let go of the brake and let the clutch out the rest of the way. You will have to gradually apply more throttle to keep the engine speed at your launch rpm. If the engine bogs, that's an indication that you need to raise your launch rpm; conversely, if the front wheel comes up too much, try a lower launch rpm. **(COURTESY OF DUCATI)**

CHAPTER 8:

Reference Points

W e briefly discussed reference points in Chapter 2 (on visual skills), but the topic is important enough that it deserves a separate chapter with more detail. A reference point is a marker—anything from an obvious cone at the side of the track to a tiny mark in the pavement—that tells you where you should be going or what you should be doing. At Daytona, for example, I used to follow the wall at the top of the banking all the way around until I got to the "A" in DAYTONA, painted on the wall. When I got to the letter, I started to come down off the top of the banking and into the tri-oval; that was my reference point.

While I'm riding around the track, just concentrating on riding and doing laps on my own, I'm always looking for a faster way. I'm always looking to hit the braking markers right, hit the apex right, get the bike turned in at the right moment, and watching

OPPOSITE: The hillsides at Brands Hatch are full of potential reference points. When you crest a blind turn, the opposite hillside is usually the first thing that comes into view; choose something that's there permanently to use as a marker. (GOLD & GOOSE)

for the outside of the track to run it out as far as I can. Ideally, you will have reference points for each of those actions, and more—a sufficient number of them around the track so that your concentration flows from one to the next without a break. Before you pass a certain marker and it goes out of sight, you've already noted the next one and are shifting your focus to it.

For example, you should have reference points to mark the turn-in point, the apex, and the exit of a particular corner. As you approach the corner, you are looking for the turn-in point, which may be a tire mark on the rumble strip at the edge of the track. But before you actually get to that marker, you should already be shifting your focus to your apex marker—perhaps the track-day provider has put a cone there. Once you're past your turn-in point and heading to the apex, you should already be looking for your exit point. Your focus should move seamlessly from one point to the next; this will require that you're able to see each marker in your peripheral vision without actually looking at it, as we discussed in Chapter 2.

If there are areas of the track where you don't have a good series of reference points to focus on, it's

easy to become lost and lose your confidence. This happens especially in blind turns, because for a brief time there is nothing to see or use for a reference point. I'll address blind turns later in the chapter, but I'm sure you've experienced that "lost" feeling when you crest a blind turn. If you get that feeling even on a part of the track where you can easily see the upcoming corner, that is a sure sign that you need more reference points in that area. Another benefit of reference points is that they help with consistency; if you have good markers in a particular section and are able to do it right just once, you'll be able to do it again and again the same way.

Some reference points are more important than others, and will require more attention. At Mugello, you're doing almost 350 kilometers per hour (220 miles per hour) on a MotoGP bike down the front straight. There's a kink and a hill at the end of the straight, and you head to the left to go over the hump, where you can just see the 200-meter board. For almost the full length of the straight, you're aiming for that board and not looking at anything else; almost all of your concentration is focused on that braking marker. Other reference points are

much less obvious, but just as important. It could be just a bit of paint on the tarmac that you know is a good spot to ride over each lap; you see it, run over it, and move on to the next point. It takes almost no concentration and is only in sight for a moment, but a few of those at different places around the track can really add to your confidence and comfort level.

While reference points are important and useful, you should not get so focused on them that you get stuck and can't adapt to changes. Your braking markers, for instance, are not where you absolutely must begin your braking every time. If you get a particularly good drive onto the straight or a slipstream one lap, you'll have to brake a bit earlier than the marker you normally use. But if you make a little mistake, you might be going slower and can brake later. Another example is a point you use to make your turn in the second part of a chicane. If you haven't done the first part perfectly, you may not want to bring the bike all the way across the track for the second part; you can cut your line one meter or so on the inside of where you normally go, because you haven't got the speed and don't have to go so wide. Things will also change as you gain experience and go more quickly; you may find you want to be at a different place on the track in a certain spot, your

OPPOSITE TOP: Ideally you will find a sufficient number of reference points around the track so that you'll have more than one in your field of view at any given time. This will help you "connect the dots" for a lap and improve consistency. (COURTESY OF DUCATI)

OPPOSITE BOTTOM: While some reference points are crucial and require a good deal of focus, others are more for personal comfort. That mark on the tarmac may be something you run over every lap, only in sight for a moment before you move on to the next point, but enough of these around the track can increase your confidence significantly. (COURTESY OF DUCATI)

turn-in points may be later, and so on.

You want to make sure that your reference points are not going to move over time. At a track day there will sometimes be cones out to make things easier, but the next time you go to that track, they may not be there, or they may be in a different spot. At some tracks I have reference points that I've used for years and years, such as the two white lines on the track at the end of the front straight at Phillip Island. Sometimes they put braking markers up there, and sometimes not, but those lines have been there forever, and I've always used them.

At a track like Brands Hatch, there are plenty of things to use on the hillsides for markers. Some of them, like a team truck, will be in the same spot all weekend, but others, maybe a hot dog stand, can move around. Things like that can change all the time, but if it just caught your eye at the right time—like when you tipped into a corner, for instance—as long as it's something that will be in the same spot all weekend, it's definitely worth taking advantage of.

A good reference point doesn't necessarily have to be something you only see; it can also be a characteristic of the track, like a bump in the tarmac. Exiting Siberia at Phillip Island, there was a little bump as I hit fourth gear at the same time as I was trying to get the bike from the left to the right for the next corner. As the bike was coming over from the left, it was hitting the bump and throwing the wheel up and making it change direction faster for me. I had to hit that little bump to get it right. I could see it, I knew where it was, and that was where I knew I had to be.

Lukey Heights at Phillip Island is a blind left-hand turn cresting a hill that leads into MG, a tight right-hander. It's a difficult section because you can't see anything, and there are no markers as you crest the hill, but you have to brake for MG right over the top. With no reference points to use, this must be done on memory and feel. A lot of guys end up being out too wide through Lukey Heights, but you need to apex in two spots. As you hit the second apex and start to drift out, you have to come over the hill in the middle of the track; for that, you have to find something you can use as a marker on the track itself, and that's the last reference point you've got before going over the hill. Cresting the hill, you can't actually see where to begin braking. When I come over the hill, I wait for the revs to hit a point that I know—and I'm not looking at the tachometer, but going by feel—then I close the

throttle and start to brake.

Blind corners on the race track are usually blind because they go over a hill. To minimize the amount of time where you don't have any reference points to focus on, try to find a spot on the track as close to the crest as you can to use as a marker, to show you where to actually go over the peak of the hill. On the other side, it's the same thing; you want to have something to focus on as early as possible after cresting the hill. That will usually be an object on a hillside in the distance, such as a tree or a building. I also like to use light poles in the distance at tracks that have a lot of elevation changes, as they are usually the first thing you're able to see over the top of a hill. You do have to be careful about using something far

away, though, because if you are even just slightly off-line, the object can appear in a different spot relative to the track.

When you end up in a group of riders, it can be very difficult to see your markers. A lot of times you're in the group and looking for your braking marker or other reference point, but you're also keeping your eye on the other guys, going with the flow; you have to go by feel, then, and it falls into more of a rhythm. Also, since you are with other riders, when you do get to your braking markers, you're not going to be doing the latest, greatest braking you can do—unless you're trying to get past. At Monza, for example, halfway down any of the long straights, you've probably got a good slipstream, but

Light poles or buildings on a hillside far away can make good markers to aim for when cresting a rise in the track. Just remember that if you are off-line even slightly, an object far away can easily steer you wrong, because it will appear to have moved quite a bit relative to where you are on the track. Looking up the front straight at Laguna Seca, **(TOP - BRIAN J. NELSON)** you can just see some light poles over the crest of turn 1. At the top of the hill, **(BOTTOM – COURTESY OF DUCATI)** they are all you can see.

Many inexperienced—and even experienced!—riders make the mistake of using another rider for a moving reference point. It's an easy way to get around the track, but once you are on your own, you'll be lost, as you won't know where you are going. In addition, if the rider you are following makes a mistake, you will likely make the same mistake. Here, Neil Hodgson, Colin Edwards, and I brake for a corner at Monza in 2002. The three of us were dicing, and I ran off the track at the end of one of the straights. Since Colin was using me for his braking marker, he ended up running off as well. **(GOLD & GOOSE)**

RIGHT: Reference points are just as important for street riding as they are on the track, but are usually used for very different reasons. On an unknown road, a tree over a corner could mean damp pavement underneath; on a road you've been on before, a particular feature may remind you that the next corner is a tricky, decreasing-radius bend. Only on roads you ride often will you gradually find markers for corner apexes, blind turns, and so on. **(ANDREW TREVITT)**

that doesn't mean you have to pass; plenty of times I've rolled off the throttle and stayed behind because I don't want to be showing everything all the time. Then it becomes more about race craft, something I'll discuss in Chapter 12.

You can, of course, get into some huge trouble if you pay too much attention to what the other riders are doing, and begin to use them as your moving reference point. One of the straights at Monza ends with a first-gear chicane, which you absolutely have to get the braking right for; I always used to brake at the 200-meter line, give or take a few meters, depending on the wind and how much of a slipstream I had on the straight. In 2002, Colin Edwards, Neil Hodgson, and I were battling there for the lead in race 1. I overshot the braking marker and couldn't get slowed down for the corner. Because Colin was following me and doing basically exactly what I was doing, he couldn't bring it in either, so he ran off with me—even though he was still five bike lengths behind me! He was using me for a marker, and we both ran off.

A big part of learning a new track is finding reference points to use. Sometimes you can walk the track and see some things, like broken bits of tarmac or marks on the curbs, but it's difficult to find many useful reference points until you get out there and ride. The speeds and your sense of distance are so different when you ride that you may not even see some of the marks you found walking the track. You've got to go out, knowing that you're going to struggle and take some time to get up to speed. But you'll see things that you can use: a building on a hillside that you aim for when cresting a rise, or a patch of dirt that marks a turn-in point. Some reference points that you use early on may not work as you get faster, so you'll have to look for different markers. It may take some time to get it right, but as you get more experience, it will become easier to recognize useful markers quickly as you get up to speed on a new track.

CHAPTER 9:

Away From the Track—Mental and Physical

Even though motorcycle races are held on the weekends, motorcycle racing is a full-time job for the riders. There are commitments to keep the sponsors happy, test days, training for both strength and stamina, finding and preparing the right food to eat . . . all that can take a lot of time. Whenever I was not at the track, I was thinking about getting myself fit and making sure I was in good condition for the next race. I was always hard on myself, and racing was always on my mind; I hardly ever slept. Even if I had won the last race, I would come home and enjoy the moment for only a couple of hours, and then I'd start training my ass off because I'd already be worrying about the next race. Even if you're not a full-time racer, what you do off the bike to improve your riding is just as important as what you do when you're on it.

> **OPPOSITE:** My set routine was always a few minutes of quiet just before the start, when I focused in on what I would have to do in the race. Even at a track day or on a street ride, you need to be in the right mind-set before you get on the bike. It may involve some time to yourself or something completely different, like a set ritual of getting suited up— whatever it takes to give you confidence in yourself. **(COURTESY OF DUCATI)**

In Chapter 1 we talked briefly about the physical and mental aspects of riding, and how they are related. Essentially, as you improve your physical condition, your stamina on the bike will also improve; you will be more consistent, and you will be able to concentrate more on your actual riding rather than being distracted by how tired you're getting. Likewise, as you improve your riding, it will be more efficient, requiring less effort and freeing up energy so that you are able to ride at your best for longer. Work on one aspect, and the other will naturally benefit, as well.

I was always (and still am) a fanatic about fitness, and I am pretty sure I was the guy who worked the hardest out of everybody. Especially as I was getting older, I had to make sure I stayed on top of my game in order to compete with the younger guys coming through. In the early years, I used to just go and wear myself out by doing too much, but later I changed a lot of my training. In the end I was quite smart about it; I was doing the right work in the gym, focusing on workouts that would cross over and improve my results on the motorbike. I like to have a balance of strength and stamina, so I combined the work in the gym with cardio on the bicycle. It's definitely easier to muscle a motorcycle around the stronger you are, but to run two superbike races in one day—or ride every session to get the most out of a track day—you will also need good stamina.

When I was living in Monaco from 2000 to the start of 2009, 20 kilometers (13 miles) down the road was a place called Ventimiglia, which is actually in Italy. I used to ride my bicycle there, do an hour or so in the gym, and then ride home. I used to do that three or four times a week, and then do a couple of longer rides on the weekend. I've always loved the bicycle, but I definitely overdid it for a while. There were times when I came back to Australia at Christmas, especially in the early days, and spent quite a bit of time on the bicycle. I sometimes used to get back to Europe weighing 64 kilograms (140 pounds), but I would be so weak that I'd hop on the motorbike and be absolutely hopeless. It was better when I was heavier. At the end of 2008 I was 70 kilograms (155 pounds), and feeling great on the bike.

In those early years I rode the bicycle a bit too much, but in 2005 I started working with Rok, a trainer that used to work with many of the professional Australian cyclists. He changed the way I did things quite a lot. We started to do really specific exercises in the gym that strengthened the muscles used for riding rather than just a general program that worked on overall strength. It really helped me, especially as I got older. Toward the end I used to do much more in the gym, as I've worn away the cushions in the discs in my back because I've been riding bicycles and motorcycles for so many years.

A lot of riders train on motocross or flat-track bikes, but I think there are a couple of disadvantages to doing so. I did that for a while, especially in the early days when I raced in the British and Australian championships. If I was ever at home I'd ride motocross on the farm, and I also did a bit of supermotard. But in 2005, when I was riding for Honda, I fell off my motocross bike and broke my wrist really badly; it was a stupid crash. We had just had a good test and my year was starting to look better, but I had been riding for hours that day and just overdid it. I fell off, broke my wrist, and missed the rest of the year. That really put me off the motocross bikes, and after that I never rode another one while I was roadracing. A lot of guys do it, but I really think it puts you in a situation where you can hurt yourself.

I also don't think riding something other than your race bike gives you much benefit. I'd hop back

on the superbike after riding the motocross bike, and I'd feel like an alien; the bikes were just too different. If you're not finding the limits like you do when you're racing, I think it's very important that you don't muck around with slow bikes in between. It's got to be full-on all the time. I haven't done any testing lately, but because I'm doing the schools and going to press launches, I think I'm teaching myself how to go slow these days. I used to like hopping off the race bike and then not riding anything else until the next race, even if it was three or four weeks

away. As soon as I hopped back on the bike, I had it fresh in my mind from the last race or test, because I hadn't ridden anything else.

The final part of your physical fitness is diet, and just as you don't have to be the fittest person in the world, you also don't have to stick to a precise diet. I always eat well; my wife Kim is a great cook, and makes all types of dishes. We may have fish and chips or a hamburger every now and again, but I hardly ever eat junk food. I'm not taking any pills, making protein shakes or the like; I eat what comes out of

OPPOSITE: Many riders like to train using motocross or supermotard bikes, but later in my career I rode nothing but the race bikes; anything else was too slow and too different to keep you sharp. When I rode nothing else, my mind stayed sharp and I felt fresh every time I hopped on the bike, even if it was a test after several weeks off. **(FOCUS PHOTOGRAPHY)**

RIGHT: Riding a bicycle is a great form of training that helps you to develop both strength and stamina. One other benefit is that it can get you away from everything and give you some much-needed time to yourself—often hard to find at the top levels of the sport. **(TROY BAYLISS)**

the fridge, in moderation. This can be difficult when you're traveling or rushed at the race track, but it's worth the effort to find a decent restaurant when you're on the road, or taking what you'll need to the track rather than relying on what they have at the stands there.

Motorcycle racing and riding is definitely more mental than physical. Of course the physical side is important, but you've got to have the right attitude and believe in yourself. I don't think I was the most talented rider in the world, but I used to believe that I was fast and I used to train hard. There have been so many races where it's been so hot that sometimes you just want to give up. At Misano, for instance, there have been times when I've been standing on the podium, nearly passing out. A lot of that was because I was following Colin Edwards or another Ducati, and when you're riding so close to one another on those twins, you've got their exhaust right in your face; it was so hard to breathe because it was so hot and you're so close. Getting through that was really hard, but I also used to think of that when I was in front and they were behind me. I was thinking, "Those guys have got to be having it so tough there." This is another way in which the mental and physical sides of racing are linked: When I was racing, I made sure I was the fittest person there; anytime during

a race when it was getting hard, I used to believe that no one could be fitter than me and that gave me another edge.

Your confidence plays such a big part in your success; if it takes that bit of extra time to relax or do something special to put you in the right frame of mind for a race, it's worth doing. This applies to riding just as much as racing. If your mind is not on what you're doing at a track day—or even if you're just riding home from work at the end of a long day—take the time to sort things out before you get on your bike.

Everybody is different when it comes to getting in the right mind-set to race. Some people need to listen to music. Others are quite superstitious about what they wear, or have to follow an exact routine leading up to the race. There are some riders who can joke around with their crew or friends and not seem at all stressed the whole race weekend. At home between races, all I was thinking about was getting myself fit and making sure I was in good condition for the next race; I didn't usually think about setup or anything to do with the actual riding of the bike. But just before a race, I liked to have 10 or 15 minutes of quiet time in the truck. I'd normally have Kim and Rok there, and we'd talk a little bit, but it was more about me just being calm and thinking about what I needed to do. It wasn't putting laps together in my head so much as thinking about the situation and focusing on what I had to do in the race.

If you look at any MotoGP or World Superbike grid, everyone who's going into that race can't be thinking that they're going to win. But when you're in a good situation—you're on a good team with a factory bike, and things are going well—that's what you have to believe. Davide Tardozzi was good at snapping me out of things. Sometimes he'd yell and scream at me and grab me by the neck. But especially in the earlier days, he used to just try and get me to believe in myself. He'd tell me how fast I was, and I believed it. Toward the end, I didn't need anyone to tell me—I was that confident in myself. When I went to a race, I thought I was unbeatable.

Confidence can work the other way just as easily, though, and it's funny what it can do to you when things aren't working out the way you want them to, even if you're in your best condition ever. When you get on a roll, it's great, and everything seems to happen easily. Sometimes I'd hop on the bike and win, and at the end of the race I'd jump off and think, "I could do that again right now—throw some tires on and let's go, no problem." But when you're not confident in your setup or what you have going on with the bike or the tire, that's not a good way to

start the race. I never used to go very well at Brno, and I'd come in absolutely wrecked from wrestling with the bike the whole race. I might end up finishing ninth, feeling like I'd had a really hard race, I was so far away. Me and my bike; sometimes we work as one, but there were a lot of times when we didn't.

Good fitness and confidence in yourself can make a huge difference when it comes to getting over an injury, or even riding while still injured. The thing is, if you're going to succeed and get to the top levels of racing, you're going to break things. You're going to find it tough; you're going to have bad things happen to you. But the things that you do to try and make yourself ready for the next race can be pretty unbelievable. In 2008 I had a crash on my bicycle just before Assen. I ended up with cuts and scrapes on my back, and was bruised in a really bad way, but I still managed to do the double that weekend. Sometimes you just can't understand how talent or fitness can get you through a particular day.

As you gain experience, you will most likely find there will be more and more distractions keeping you from thinking about your riding. Your bike will need more attention to set up, there will be fans at the race track, you will have to interact with the people helping you, and you will have more things to worry about. It's important to keep these things

separate and not lose track of what's most important: your riding.

At my level, the PR commitments and distractions are all part of it; one just rolls into the other because it's always happening simultaneously. I could be in my 10-minute zone or sitting in my chair on the grid, and then all of a sudden the boss from Ducati would come by with someone he wanted me to meet. You've got to be able to handle it all and just roll with it, however it ends up going.

This is another benefit of bicycling: It gets you away from everybody. There weren't many of us bicycling when I was doing it, but now everyone seems to do hundreds of miles. This not only makes you good and strong, but it also gets you away from the stressful side of racing, and really frees up your mind. You may have a lot of pressure—a lot of sponsors to satisfy, and obligations to fulfill—but when you're on your bicycle, you're able to just get away from everything. In the gym you're around others, and although it may be pretty quiet, people can still come in and distract you when you just want to do your own thing. On a bicycle, you can go into the mountains and be alone for hours.

Even after all the physical preparation, the stress and worrying and the long hours in the shop, you can still just have a bad day. Darrell Healey, my old boss in the GSE squad, and my manager for a long time, used to joke that I had a twin brother named Kevin who couldn't ride at all. He was always with Kim watching the races, and if I was having a bad day, he'd say, "Ah, looks like we've got Kevin riding the bike today."

You do have good days and bad days, but the thing is, you want to have a *lot* of good days. Lately, everyone wants to know what's going on inside your head, and everything is getting more serious. Back in the day when I first started riding for Kawasaki in Australia, if I was struggling or having trouble, I had this mechanic who would say, "Just go and get a pie into you. You just need a pie." Sometimes you need to go outside the circle and free your mind of all the non-riding parts; you need to do whatever it takes to make every day a good day.

CHAPTER 10:

Rain and Extreme Conditions

When I was racing at home in Australia, I hardly ever rode in the rain. But when I first went to England in 1998, it was a massive change in the weather for me.

At my very first race weekend, it was pouring down with rain the first time I got on the bike. After a couple of years in England, I had faced all the bad conditions you could ever imagine: I rode with snow on the track at Donington, in temperatures below freezing, in rain with temperatures only just above freezing . . . I quickly understood how you have to prepare, especially for the cold. Riding in the rain—or in any extreme weather—is a lot about dressing appropriately and keeping comfortable so that you can concentrate on your riding without being distracted. But it's also about confidence, and having experience with all sorts of conditions.

A lot of the English riders and the older guys

OPPOSITE: While it's clearly raining a lot here at Silverstone in 2007, when you are on the track it can be difficult to tell just how much rain is falling. On a long, fast straight, a sprinkle can seem like a downpour. You can best tell in the slow corners how bad conditions are, or by looking at what puddles are forming. **(GOLD & GOOSE)**

who have been around for a while are all quick in the rain. There are always a few standout guys who just fly in tricky conditions; as soon as it starts raining, somehow they find their confidence and away they go. But really, most of the top guys are pretty rapid in the rain, as they end up riding in it a lot of the time. For me, because I hadn't done too much of that, it took some time to get it together. It's just one of those things that you have to experience and do regularly to stay sharp.

If you're living in an area where you'll be riding in conditions that are generally cool or where you'll have regular rain, you'll need riding gear—boots, gloves, leathers, or jacket and pants—that isn't perforated. This will help keep you warm, but unperforated gear will also stop the water from coming straight in on you. Of course, you can also wear a rain suit, which will stop both the wind and rain from coming in. You'll also need some warm undergarments, like a non-vented undersuit, and something to protect your neck. There is nothing more distracting than cold rainwater running inside your leathers. Your hands, feet, and chest are the most important areas to keep warm. Most apparel companies offer cold-weather gear that is waterproof or lined, but sometimes it can be pretty restrictive; I've used a bit of plastic and even newspaper down my chest, and that is often just enough to take the wind off. In the really extreme cold, I've worn surgical gloves under my regular gloves.

At the other end of the spectrum, in hot weather you'll want everything perforated—undersuit, gloves, leathers, and boots. There's not too much you can do in these conditions because you still have to wear all your gear, so it's important to keep your core temperature as low as you can. I'd always take a really cold shower as late as possible before the race, and on the start line, I'd have a wet towel to try and keep cool. Later on in my career, I didn't handle the heat as well as I did when I was younger; it was difficult for me, and I didn't enjoy riding in the heat so much. Many times I would hop off the bike and feel like I was going to pass out. The sooner you can get out of your gear and cool off after a session on the track, the better.

I used to get in trouble because sometimes before I went to the podium, I would go and get my leathers off and just put on some team kit. After the podium there would be a press conference, and then the paddock show, so keeping my gear on meant being stuck in hot, sweaty leathers for another hour in 38- or 40-degree heat (100 to 104 degrees Fahrenheit). I'd have to be ready for the second race, so even though

it sometimes meant getting in trouble, I'd go and get changed anyway.

At the top level, riders are lucky enough to have a complete second set of gear. If my gloves or leathers got wet from the rain or from sweating in the heat, I would put on fresh, dry gear for the next race. If you have that option, it makes a big difference, especially in the rain. Once you actually get going, you really don't get that wet. You catch the spray from other bikes and the rain when you're going slow or waiting on the grid, but the faster you go, the more the rain just rolls right off you.

In the heat, cold, or rain, the time to be careful is when you actually stop riding and come into the pits. Even if you're a track-day rider waiting for your next session, it's then that you feel the heat or cold the most. If you're riding in the heat, the wind will help you to cool off a bit; in the cold, the activity will warm you up. But if you get overheated or too cold between sessions, rather than trying to keep yourself comfortable and ready to ride, you will definitely have trouble once you get back on the bike.

There are many different things you can do to get ready for riding in the rain, but the most important is to properly prepare your helmet visor. On the outside I used Rain-X; you can just turn your head for half a second on a fast straight and the water rolls right

off. But everyone's had fog or water on the inside of their visor, which can make it impossible to see properly. I never said anything about it during my career, because you never want to complain about the helmet sponsor, but every now and then I had a problem, just as everyone else has. A lot of times I used a FogCity insert on the inside of my visor to stop the fogging, and sometimes I even put duct tape down from my nose, just to make sure that nothing was going to happen.

On the start line of the race, I would have Kim making sure that my helmet was looked after so that no rain would go inside and on the visor; there is nothing worse than that, because it just sits there and you can't wipe it off—although of course you're tempted. When I did get a bit of fog, I'd just lift the visor half a centimeter on a straight to let some air in. You can only do your best to prepare for that sort of thing; it will happen sometimes, and you just have to deal with it as best you can.

As I said, riding well in the rain comes from experience and confidence, because you don't have as much feel for what's going on as you do in the dry. When you're riding around the track at 180 kilometers per hour (110 miles per hour), it can look like it's really raining when you see it on your visor, even though it may be just a sprinkle. You've got to take

into consideration how much rain is coming down, and you can see that best in the slow corners rather than judging by what's happening on the straights. By the time you see puddles, it's pretty wet, but when it first starts raining, you can still go fast for quite a while.

Sometimes, when there was a light sprinkle, I remember my dad saying to me, "It's all in your head; you can go out there and still do the lap time." Normally I would get faster every session until I had a moment or crashed, because you just can't feel the bike as well as you can in the dry.

The most difficult thing is finding the limit with the front brake at the ends of the straights. Some tracks are much worse than others, but that is normally what catches people out; usually there is just no grip there because the cars brake so hard and make the tarmac smooth. That, and highsides on the exits of the corners, are the most common crashes in the wet.

If you can get your knee down in the corners, that will lift your confidence up so much because you will feel more like you're riding in the dry; you've got the feeling that you can lean the bike over. A lot of riders put an extra knee slider on so that it's easier to do that, because obviously, you won't be able to get the bike over as you normally would. A lot of it depends on the track; if you're on a track where you can get some grip, you can actually get close to how you would normally

If you can get your knee down in the rain, this will really boost your confidence, as it will feel more like you're riding normally. Many riders put double-thickness knee sliders on in the rain for just that reason, as I've done here. Note that I've also got duct tape over my nose to make sure my visor doesn't fog up. **(COURTESY OF DUCATI)**

ride. Assen is usually very good in the rain. There are some places where I would enjoy riding the track in the rain, like Brands Hatch—although there was not a lot of room for error, and it wasn't very safe. Then there are some tracks, like Le Mans or Magny-Cours, that don't have much grip. And Monza has a lot of trees that hang over the edges of the track in Lesmo 1 and 2, and make it dodgy.

Even though you're trying to get that feeling of your knee on the ground, as you normally would, riding in the rain is all about trying not to lean over too much. The more you lean the bike over, the easier it is to lose the rear end with even the lightest touch of the throttle. You have to be as smooth as you can with every control input. When you get on the gas, you have to be gentle. Instead of grabbing the front brake, you're squeezing it. And you have to be lighter with your steering inputs, especially in a chicane. I like to think of it as trying to walk across dry leaves without breaking them—you have to be that light on everything, and pay that much attention to what you're doing. Eventually you get into a rhythm; it's like you're doing everything in slow motion compared to how you would normally ride in the dry. It requires very little physical effort, but it takes a lot of concentration in every corner, and can be mentally tiring. It sometimes feels like every lap in the rain is a qualifying lap.

There are often strange situations where it's half wet or half dry, or you end up with slicks in a downpour; they can be really difficult to deal with. The worst is when the track has a dry line but is still mostly wet. If it's declared a dry race, you're starting off on slicks. That puts you in a difficult position when there is only one line; to make a pass, you've got to go off the dry line and into the wet. It's almost the same as when it just starts to rain. You have to just have the confidence and believe that you can do it. When the track is just getting wet, or drying out after it stops raining, it comes down to knowing the track and how it reacts to the rain. Those conditions aren't much fun, and sometimes it doesn't work out and you have a crash. However, if you want to get the experience necessary to ride better in the rain, you really need to do it in these difficult conditions—even though you know you're playing with fire.

Half the battle of riding in the rain, heat, or cold is just being prepared with the proper gear so that you can concentrate fully on your riding and not worry about being comfortable. Another big part of it is experience; take whatever opportunities you can to ride in those tricky conditions when there's no pressure, so that when you *do* have to ride in the heat, rain, or cold, you'll be as ready as you can be.

CHAPTER 11:
Setup

Racers, especially at the World and National Championship levels, are always looking for ways to go faster. Before (and even during) every session on the track, mechanics will make adjustments or even fit different parts, all in a search for the setup that best suits that particular track on that particular day. Those championship-level riders have a small army of mechanics and engineers to keep track of all the changes. The team will have notebooks and laptop computers filled with data from previous races to refer to, and most likely there are two riders who can compare notes. Although club racers and track-day riders don't have those same luxuries, there is a lot that can be learned from the big-team approach to setup.

Here, when I talk about *setup*, I am referring to anything on your bike that you can adjust to affect its performance: suspension, ride heights, footpeg and handlebar position, EFI settings, rake or offset . . . .

OPPOSITE: Document as much information as possible about the adjustments you make, along with the conditions and how the changes affected your bike. This will help you return to a known setup if you stray too far. (COURTESY OF DUCATI)

Even on a stock bike there are plenty of adjustments you can make. The great irony in setup is that when things are going well, you never have to change much; if you're winning your races or lapping well at your track day, there's no need to mess with the settings. But if you're struggling mid-pack or off your usual pace, it can be a constant battle, trying to find the problem. It's easy to go down the wrong path; sometimes you start changing things and it just turns into a fight with the bike, and even your crew. With each change, you lose more confidence because you're not used to what you're riding. At worst, you end up not even understanding what you've done, or how you got there.

The great thing about today's motorcycles is that, compared to even just a few years ago, they are really good stock, and you can go quite fast on them without changing a thing. When I first rode World Superbike on the 996, there was a huge difference in horsepower between the superbike and the street bike—even the R version; the street bike would be way off the lap times at the track. But in the last few years it has tightened up incredibly, even the power gap. You can jump on the R model or the homologated race version of the Panigale and lap within two or three seconds of a competitive superbike lap time, and there's hardly any difference at all between the latest Panigale and the Superstock bike.

For track-day riders and even beginning club racers, this means you don't have to worry as much about having the latest bits or trick parts; the best thing you can do is keep good tires on your bike and go ride. That way you can concentrate more on your riding and making the most of the adjustments the stock bike does have.

Of course, we all love to play with the bike and make changes, and racers especially will eventually need to make some modifications. The key here is to avoid changing too much at any one time, whether it's a setup change or a new part; at each step, you have to find decent base settings that you can go back to, even if they are not optimum. This applies to tires and maintenance as well: Try to stick with one brand and model of tire, keeping the pressures set correctly, and keeping an eye on things like your steering head bearings, suspension linkage, and the condition of your brake fluid and fork oil. Everything must be in good working order to keep your bike working as consistently as possible.

When you're changing stuff so often and so much, or if your bike is changing over time as something wears out, you won't get comfortable enough with any single setup to make the most of it. It will be difficult to find the confidence to give that last little bit of effort to get your riding to the next level. On the flip side of the "try not to change too much" argument, you *do* have to experiment with the adjustments on your bike if you're going to learn what they do and how they will affect your bike.

On the factory Ducati team, I had two important people looking after setup. The first was Ernesto Marinelli, my engineer. He has been around a long time, working with Ben Bostrom, Anthony Gobert, and all the Ducati riders in the United States. I worked with Ernesto when I rode in America, and when I left for the World Superbike Championship, I wanted him to come with me; unfortunately, it wasn't possible. Ernesto really understood where I was coming from; he's an engineer, but he's not scared to have a go at something different, and is brilliant as far as setup goes. When I returned to Ducati in 2006, I was able to work with Ernesto until I retired.

Then I had my electronics engineer, Alessandra Balducci, who I have spoken of previously. She was with me from 2006 as well, and looked after the traction control and fuel injection settings. Alessandra was always asking me how the bike felt, and my biggest complaint was always the first throttle opening; I wanted it as smooth as I could get it. But

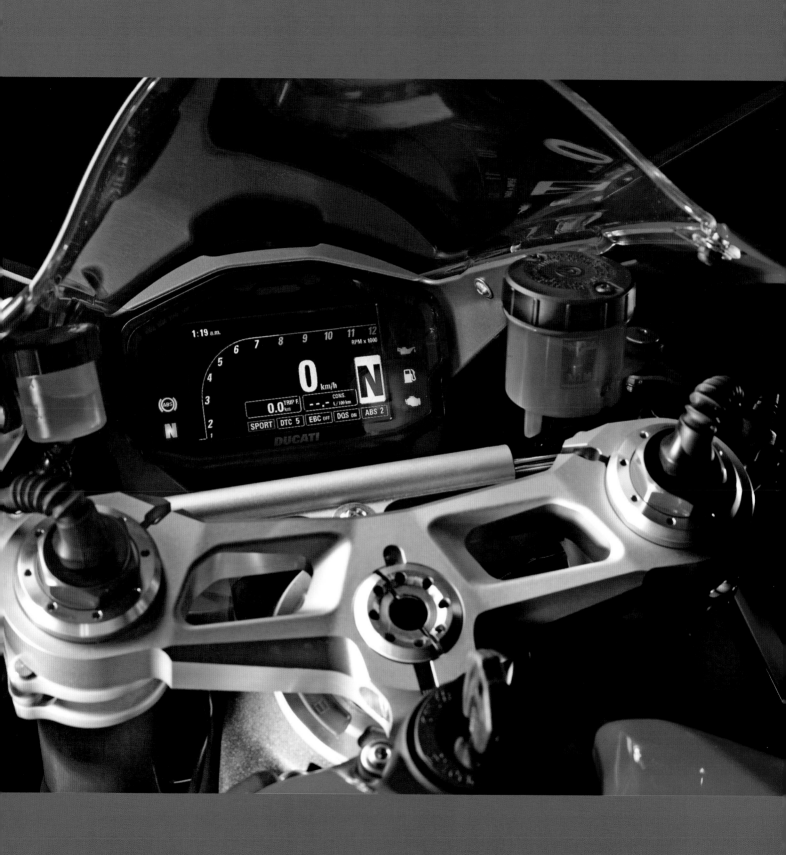

On the one hand, sticking with a base setup and not venturing far from it allows you to concentrate more on your riding and have some confidence to get to the next level. But on the other hand, if you don't make changes to your setup, you won't learn what those changes do, and how to improve your bike. Either way, when the race starts, you have to deal with whatever setup you have and make the most of it. **(COURTESY OF DUCATI)**

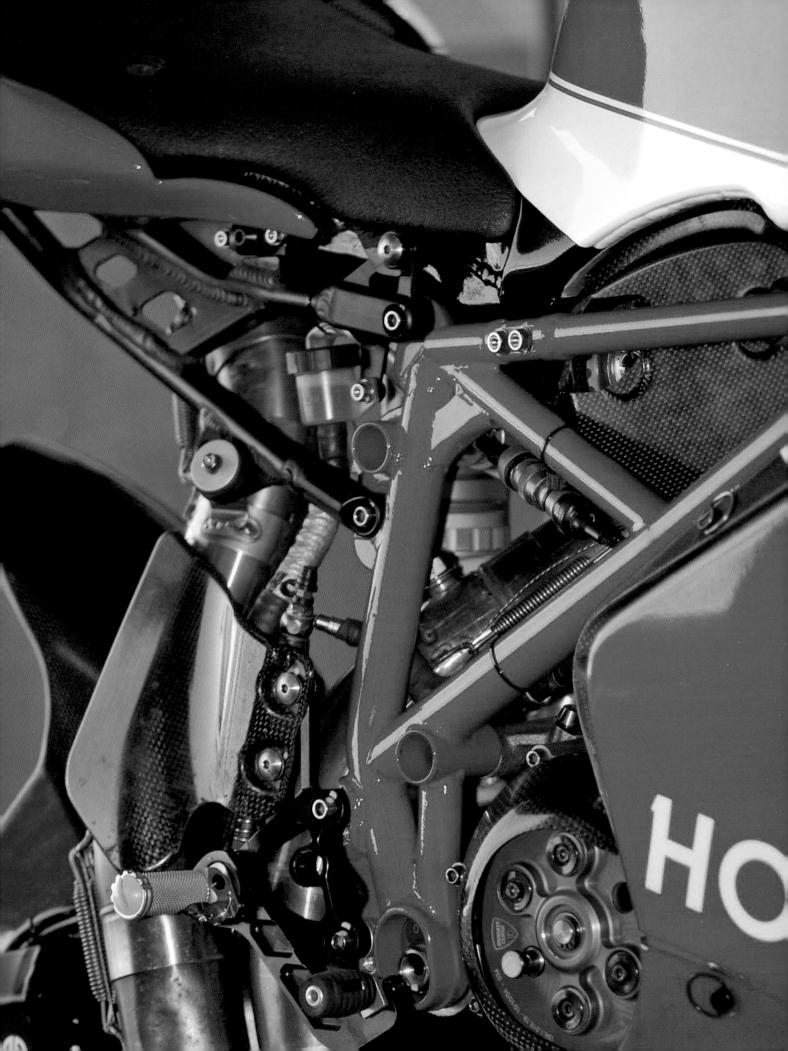

a lot of times she was doing things with the engine and traction control without even asking me. She could see on the computer what was happening, she knew what we were looking for, and could do all of that on her own.

Then, of course, there are plenty of other people on the team: a number of mechanics to work on the bikes, a parts manager, and so on. We also had a tire technician, but I knew the Pirellis quite well, and we always knew pretty much what we were going to be running.

Everyone on the team played an important role, but Alessandra and Ernesto were the two essential people when it came to setup.

Early on in my World Superbike career, we were changing the setup quite a lot. We were always swapping front discs, for example; 310, 315, or 320mm, or 290mm ventilated. I was a little bit lost then, as I didn't have much experience, but by the time I came back in 2006, and we found a base setup I liked, we didn't change the bike too much at all. We had one disc, the 320mm, and that was it. We found a good offset and head angle that was comfortable for me, and hardly ever changed that. Basically we'd change a few clicks here, a few clicks there, and no more than half a kilo on a spring. Even if we went to a new track, we would start with our base settings. I would

have to learn the track first, and then we would start from there with gearing; that is pretty much always the first thing to work on. Then, it would usually be spring rate, depending on how much grip the track had. Normally, our bike setup would be good for just about any track within the last second and a half.

We even found something that worked for the rear suspension link, which many people change a lot. I always used a regressive link. As the rear suspension went down, it never got hard; it retained the same stiffness, or a bit less. The Ducati road bikes have progressive links, so as the suspension goes down, it's getting stiffer to account for a pillion passenger. A lot of the guys use a flat link, which still gets a bit harder in the travel, but not as much as the stock link. I went the other way, with a regressive link, which hardly anyone else used. It would make the bike a bit lazy, as the back would sit down a bit. Even though it was a harder bike to ride and took more physical effort, I liked it, because it really used to look after the tire, and was good for race distance. Ernesto was really brilliant with all the geometries and that aspect of setup.

In general, we changed gearing and the wheelbase more than anything. A lot of that is for the balance of the bike, because you're changing the weight distribution quite a bit when you move the rear wheel forward or rearward in the swingarm. Making the bike shorter normally makes it flick from side to side a lot easier, but it also makes it want to wheelstand a bit more. With a less-powerful bike, it's not affected as much, but if you look at a MotoGP bike, they are quite long, with very long swingarms. At a track like Portimão, where you are changing direction a lot, it's good to have the bike a bit shorter for that reason. It can get unstable under the brakes, and slides will happen quicker; you've got to be more on your toes, as they won't

be nice, progressive slides, but, rather, snappy ones. And, of course, as soon as you bring the rear wheel forward, it's the same as putting a stiffer spring in the back, which changes a lot of things as well, depending on the grip.

Sometimes we'd end up nearly back where we started, because it always takes a while to get up to speed; you have to understand that the track may not be in good condition, or there may not be enough rubber down. Normally a track will get better as the weekend goes on, and if you try and make the bike better for conditions on Friday morning, it may not work later in the weekend as the track improves. Mugello, for instance, is a place where the track can change quite a bit. You may be a second or a second and a half off what you've done before, and it's not happening, so you start playing around with the settings. You may try things, but because the track is just not that fast, it's easy to lose your way, all for the sake of nothing.

You also have to keep in mind that your bike must work well over race distance, or for a full day of riding at a track day or in the mountains, rather than just one quick lap. Some riders have their bikes set up stiff and really direct; while they are always very strong in qualifying, a bike set up like this is not as capable of doing the race distance as

BELOW: While professional teams seem to be constantly working on setup, the ideal situation is not to have to make major changes; with a good base setup, you will only have to make minor adjustments. **(GOLD & GOOSE)**

my bikes were. The regressive link was just a part of that on my setup.

One major mistake that I see a lot of people making, even street riders and track-day riders on stock bikes, is that they think they must have the back of the bike high and the front low, as that makes it easier to steer. But there are a lot of trade-offs in stability, rear grip, tire life, and so on. That type of setup may work better for a couple of laps, but at the end of the day, you're worn out from the instability, and your tires are done.

As I said earlier in the chapter, it's difficult to get into that ideal situation where you don't have to change much with your setup; everything has to be going well, and you have to be winning your races or going faster than your friends at a track day. If someone is a lot faster than you, you have to ask yourself, "What's going on? What's different? Have they found something that works?" You can't blame yourself; at that point, you have to start trying different things to find some speed.

Again, it's important to keep a baseline setting that you know works well, which you can go back

to, and then change just one thing at a time. If you change more than one thing and the bike is better or worse, you won't know which change made the difference. At every step of the way, keep good notes of what you've done and how it affected the bike. Eventually you will build up a good database, and you'll know exactly how each change affects your bike, and what to do in almost any situation.

When it comes to crunch time, a lot of it is in your head. The biggest thing that affects the lap time on the bike is the rider, and if you lose your way with the setup, it can really affect your confidence in your riding. Things can easily go from bad to worse, especially if you've strayed far from your baseline and haven't kept track of what you've done. You can do a whole heap of work, changing everything, but some days you wake up and you're just not there; it's the nut behind the handlebars that needs the attention.

OPPOSITE: At a track day, you want a setup that is comfortable enough to ride the whole day, and doesn't wear you or the tires out in just a few laps. Racers are not as worried about comfort or tire life, but you should work toward finding the best setup for full race distance rather than just one qualifying lap. **(COURTESY OF DUCATI)**

BOTTOM: Ernesto and I working hard on setup at Brno in 2008. I used to struggle a lot at Brno, but in the end I did very well there; in 2008, I won both races. Finding the right setup is difficult; sometimes if you're not doing well, you start changing things just for the sake of changing them, and it can go quickly downhill from there. **(GOLD & GOOSE)**

In the end, a top rider can—and sometimes has to—ride around quite a few things. There are so many different things that can throw a spanner in the works; just an out-of-round tire, for example. The tire can spin on the rim, putting the wheel out of balance, and then you have chatter. Once you go out for the sighting lap and the lights go green, the setup that you've been working on the whole weekend is what you've got for the race, and you've got to get through it. If you're not comfortable on it, and not confident, sometimes you've just got to say "I'm going to ride to what I can do on this, and settle for a finish and some points," or you have to say "I'm going to try and ride around it, and I don't care if

I crash." I've been there plenty of times; when you want to win, and you're not far off the pace but know you're struggling and riding overboard, that's when it gets difficult and frustrating.

Just like your riding skills evolve over time, so will your setup. As your riding improves, you may find that you prefer a different position on the bike, for example, or perhaps a change in geometry for more feel from one end of the bike than the other. And tires, bikes, and tracks are changing all the time. The people working on the Ducati Superbike team are always building and trying different things; the last time I rode the bike, Ernesto had me try a new shock with quite a different setting on the slow-speed compression, and I liked it straightaway. There are riders who like one particular thing so much, they'll stay on it and not want to try anything else, but I always tried to be more open-minded than that. As long as I got the feeling I was looking for from the bike, especially in the front end, I didn't mind trying something new.

CHAPTER 12:
Race Craft

Throughout this book I have stressed that your riding, whatever level you're at, must be second nature so that you don't have to think about each skill or the actual mechanics of what you're doing. Braking, steering, line selection, throttle control . . . it must all be done on an unconscious level. When you're riding on the street, this lets you focus more on the traffic around you and allows you to be more alert to potential dangers; rather than having to focus on *how* to turn the bike to avoid a wayward car, for example, you want to be able to concentrate entirely on *where* to go. As a track-day rider, the more automatic each skill becomes, the more you can think about other, new skills to master.

For racers, the ideal situation is to not have to think at all about your riding, so that you can focus entirely on one thing: winning the race. Race craft—

playing out a battle—is the most important skill to get right. When you're running down in eighth or ninth place, all you're doing is riding as fast as you can. But when you get close to the front and are regularly in the lead group, it becomes much different and more like a game of chess: You can play the game and use your brain. At the top level in World Superbike, all the riders are fast and all the bikes are fairly equal; in many races I'd try to put together a few laps early and see if I could make a gap, but there were not many races where I could manage to do that. It nearly always ends up with just two or three riders at the front for the last few laps, and more often than not, it's race craft that determines who wins the race rather than outright riding skill or speed.

I would always start a race with a plan in my head—an ideal way for the race to play out. Obviously, I would try and get a good start, and if I was in the front group once the race was under way, that was Plan A, already working. I would just make sure I stayed with the lead group until mid-distance; at that point, you've got to start thinking a bit more. If someone came past me, normally I wouldn't go straight back past; I'd sit and watch them for a few laps, or even longer, to see what they would have

OPPOSITE: At the beginning of a race there may be four or five riders in the lead battle, but by two-thirds distance, it is usually down to a battle of two, possibly three riders. If you are in that part of it, race craft is more often than not what decides the outcome of the race; you're in the game and playing to win. **(COURTESY OF DUCATI)**

OPPOSITE: Your setup and tire choice can make a big difference in how a race plays out, along with the race craft you use. Use a tire that's softer rather than faster over a few laps, for example, and you may end up struggling even to stay in the lead group late in the race, let alone make a play for the win. (GOLD & GOOSE)

to show. At the same time, I didn't want anyone following me for too long, and I didn't want to show my own hand.

After two-thirds of the race I'd try to get in front, because if the race was stopped, it would be declared complete. Usually at that point, the lead group would be down to two, possibly three riders, with a gap on the rest of the field. If you're in that part of it, you're in the game to win. Again, without showing too much, I would put two or three laps together and try to pull a gap; back in the day it was usually me and Colin at the front, and it was very rare that I could pull a gap on him. It was very hard for us to break one another like that, and we knew it was between the two of us. Many times, I'd save my best for the second- or third-to-last lap, and the second-to-last lap would normally be my fastest lap of the race; I'd treat it like Superpole. That's how I tried to have every race go.

At the same time all this is going on, and you have that plan in your mind, you also have to take into consideration what's happening during the race; it could all change at any time. If somebody gets a false neutral and runs wide into the gravel trap, you know you've got a couple of seconds. If you can maintain that gap to the end, you are set. There are so many things like that, the smallest little mistakes

that can contribute, and you've got to be aware of these things. This means perhaps making a pass on a straight when you get a good slipstream, even though you may not be ready to go in front, or it may mean changing the plan completely and trying to make a break from the group when another rider makes a mistake. Backmarkers can always play a big part in a race; it's all about getting around slower riders fast, and in a way that works to your advantage. You want to make it so that you get through and the riders behind you can't. Sometimes you might just be able to make the pass, and if you know that you can squeeze in there and the rider behind you can't, that gives you half a second to a second, and it will help break the group up a little bit.

When you're riding in a tight group, things can work against you just as easily. You may get stuck behind a slower rider, or somebody could bump into you. In an instant you could be down a couple of seconds from the lead group, and you've got to put in some qualifying laps to get back in the game. Sometimes when you do get separated from the lead group and have a large gap to the next rider, the temptation is there to cruise around to the finish. But, as my team manager, Davide Tardozzi, would always say to me, never give up. If you're in third position and something happens

The ideal goal is for your riding to be entirely second nature, and to not require any attention, so that you can concentrate fully on strategy to win the race. That said, you can find out some amazing things about your riding during a race, even though you are not consciously trying to work on your riding. When I won the MotoGP race at Valencia in 2006, I didn't use much strategy or race craft; I got a really good start, put my head down, and was just basically riding flat out for the entire race. That was one of those days where everything just fell into place. **(COURTESY OF DUCATI)**

at the front, there's always a chance you can end up one, or even two, spots better.

There are so many people that I raced with week in and week out, so I knew them well and was quite comfortable racing in close quarters. For instance, I spent many years with Nori Haga. We had some incredibly big races, but we never actually crashed together—although we nearly did quite a few times! Nori used to ride behind me and nearly rub my rear tire, but when he was there, I never thought about him running into me. Sometimes we'd touch, but I knew he was there and it didn't faze me—I trusted him. At Lausitzring, there was a really long right-hand corner where the rumble strip finished early, on the second part of the apex. I used to put my knee in the dirt right there, and that would really put a lot of crap up; I used to do that to Nori all the time there because I knew he was right behind me.

understood how Nori rode, and he understood how I rode; when it came down to playing it out for the race win, there were things that I would look for that could give me an advantage or could work against me. Most of the people I raced against, I just knew how they raced. I'd play games with them, and I'm sure they played games with me. Even sometimes in practice or qualifying, you end up with somebody on-track. They see you there, give it a bit of a go, then roll out of it and let you have a go. You each get a bit of an idea of where you're at, but again, you don't show everything.

When I was young, my dad always used to tell me to never look around. I didn't for a long time, but later, I always used to drop one hand and have a good look over my shoulder to see what was going on, especially near the end of the race. In the slower corners I could hear other riders behind me, depending on the bike. And then I'd also have a read of other people's pit boards on the front straight. Between all that, I'd be able to work out what was going on behind. It's important to know what's playing out behind you, because even though you may see plus-naught on your pit board, that gap could grow to as much as half a second in the half lap after you see your board. If you can have a look over your shoulder, you'll know what the gap is at exactly that moment; the difference is that with a plus-naught gap, you have to cover your line, and that will slow the pace down by easily that half a second in the next half a lap. If the gap is really half a second, you don't have to cover the line as much as you may have thought you needed to.

When I knew the race was going to be a big battle down to the last two or three laps, I wouldn't want to be leading halfway through the race; I'd always make sure to find spots where the other riders were slower or weaker. Sometimes I'd wave other riders through, so that I could have a look at them and see what they were doing. It would only take rolling off the throttle the tiniest bit on the exit of a corner, and a lot of people wouldn't even really notice it. Of

course, this came back to bite me at Brands Hatch in 2006. Nori and I were in good form, and I had already let him by once and passed him back. But I wanted to sit behind him for another few laps in the middle of the race to have a look at him, and then pass him again near the end of the race. But he had me covered, and I couldn't get back past! My plan backfired that day.

Colin and I used to have some really big battles. I never said much to any of the guys, but we always knew we were in for a battle. Ben Bostrom, Ruben Xaus, and Neil Hodgson were usually in there as well. There were times that Dunlop was on a roll, and Colin and I were struggling on the Michelins; we were just so close sometimes, but it was a bit of a tire war, and we'd just have to hang on and know it was going to turn around sooner or later.

I used to enjoy it when there were different tires; now, you know everyone's in the same boat. Back then, the tires could play a big part in how the race panned out. Tires and the setup of your bike can affect how it performs over race distance, and by mid-distance you usually have a good idea of how your bike's working compared to the others. It usually comes down to the tire you chose for the race, or the way your bike was set up, and you're always looking for the smallest things and the tiniest mistakes. I could

tell when Colin was having even the slightest bit of front tire trouble, for example, and he could see if I was having any problems; this is another reason why it's so important to have a setup that works over full race distance.

The most stressful weekend of my life was at Imola in 2002, the final round in that year's championship. It actually all started three weeks before, at Assen, when we were struggling with the bike and had chatter. In the first race I ran wide, dicing with Neil; that put me off-line, and I lost the lead group. Still, I was able to get back to second at the finish. In the second race I was again dicing with Neil, but this time I ran off into the grass at the last chicane and lost a lot of places, and then crashed trying to catch the leaders. If I hadn't run into the grass or crashed at Assen, I would have had a good cushion of points going into the last round at Imola; instead, I was one point behind Colin. On top of that, Imola was the Castrol Honda team's test track at the time, so they were already going really well there. I went there knowing what I had to do, and it was a big battle all weekend between Colin and me.

In the first race, I was just 0.7 seconds behind Colin when it was stopped with a red flag. They restarted the race and I beat Colin on-track in the second part, but I needed to beat him by at least that gap to actually win the race, as it was scored on combined time. To win the championship in race 2, I had to win and have someone finish between Colin and me—one of the most difficult positions to be in as far as race craft goes. I did the best I could; we had an incredible race and swapped the lead many times, but Colin won the race, and the championship. It would have been nice to win, but honestly, it was a good day for everybody. The best man won on the day. Everybody wants to see a battle to the finish, and they did. Colin really finished off the year strong, with nine wins in a row. I had an incredible start to the year and won many races, but it just goes to show, it's never over 'til it's over. Using race craft is fun when you really feel like you are in control of the situation and think you've got it covered, but sometimes it just doesn't work out the way you want.

Afterword

I rode my last World Superbike race at Portimão in 2008, but I'm still very involved with racing, Ducati, and the motorcycle industry. I have tested occasionally for the factory, and I have fun with the Ducati Riding Experience and my own Troy Bayliss Academy. We are in the planning stages for the second Troy Bayliss Classic, a flat-track event in my hometown of Taree that features Australian motorcycling legends. It was a huge success in its first year. Kim and I have also launched our own MOTO EXPO shows in Brisbane and Melbourne. And, of course, I have written this book.

If there is one thing that I have learned from writing this book it's that you never forget what you've learned about riding a motorcycle. Even now when I hop on the bike, I am always thinking and never taking anything for granted; I always use the experience that I've gained to understand what a track or road will be like, or how the bike will

OPPOSITE: Monza, 2008. Even though I struggled in both races, I was happy to take a podium in Race 1 and extend my points lead over the weekend. **(COURTESY OF DUCATI) RIGHT:** On the podium at the Lausitzring in 2007, after a great battle with Nori for the win in Race 2. **(COURTESY OF DUCATI)**

react. After all this time, I still use everything I've learned—everything that I've included in this book.

I've shared all of my "secret" tips about racing, but in the end, there are no shortcuts; it's an experience thing. You have to experience the riding, you have to have the crashes, and you have to undergo all the hard times in order to get to the top. It would be nice if there actually was a secret, but I'm afraid there isn't one. You can't rush it. There will always be room for improvement, but it has to come from hours and hours of practice.

t's funny how everything for me has come full circle. I had the best bikes and the best people around me, and now I find myself right back at the beginning. My youngest boy Ollie has been racing karts and has recently switched to bikes. I'm really happy about this, because now we go away and race together. With kart racing, I was always working on the kart and watching him, but now we can ride together, and it's much more fun. I support him, and he supports me. I'm back at the start, and it's just us and the bike, parked in the dirt at the track.

All of the effort and time that goes into the testing, the DRE and my own Academy, the Troy Bayliss Classic, and now the shows—it can definitely feel like work sometimes. But whenever I hop on the bike, or when Ollie and I race together or go to the flat track, there is no pressure; for me, it's all about having fun and riding with the guys.

I think it just goes to show that I must love bikes if I'm doing it all again from the start. No matter where you are in your learning curve, I hope the techniques you've learned from this book will provide you with some guidance as you continue to gain experience. Most importantly, I hope that you'll enjoy the ride along the way.

The publisher and authors would like to
thank the following photographers, who
provided their images courtesy of Ducati:

MotoGP – Photo Milagro

SBK – Fabrizio Porrozzi/StudioZAC

DRE – Andrea Bardi

Ducati Advertising – Paul Barshon